Fossiling in Florida

Mark Renz

Marisa Renz

FOSSILING

IN

FLORIDA

A Guide for Diggers and Divers

Mark Renz

Illustrations by Marisa Renz

University Press of Florida

Gainesville · Tallahassee · Tampa · Boca Raton · Pensacola · Orlando · Miami · Jacksonville

04 03 02 01 00 99 6 5 4 3 2 1

Library of Congress Cataloging-in-Publication Data

Renz, Mark.
Fossiling in Florida: a guide for diggers and divers / Mark Renz; illustrations by Marisa Renz.
p. cm.
Includes bibliographical references.
ISBN 0-8130-1677-0 (pbk.: alk. paper)
1. Fossils—Florida—Collection and preservation. I. Title.
QE747.F6R46 1999
560'.9759'075—dc21 99-17917

The University Press of Florida is the scholarly publishing agency for the State University System of Florida, comprised of Florida A & M University, Florida Atlantic University, Florida International University, Florida State University, University of Central Florida, University of Florida, University of North Florida, University of South Florida, and University of West Florida.

University Press of Florida
15 Northwest 15th Street
Gainesville, FL 32611-2079
http://www.upf.com

To the amateur in us all

Contents

Forewords

Florida has a particularly subtle way of yielding up its fossil wealth. In the late nineteenth century, this state's vertebrate paleontological resources remained unknown even after the western expeditions of Ferdinand Vandiveer Hayden, Othniel Charles Marsh, and Edward Drinker Cope had opened up the great Tertiary basins of the western interior.

Finally in the late 1880s, just as the dinosaur rush burst upon the Rocky Mountain region, a couple of handfuls of intriguing fossils from the Peace River and from the Ocala limerock crevice found their way into the able hands of Dr. Joseph Leidy of the Philadelphia Academy of Natural Sciences.

Even now, on the threshold of a new millennium, astonishing new finds continue to show up in unexpected places in Florida. Although we have grown past the pioneer stage of paleontological exploration, we certainly live in an exciting era of discovery. This low-lying landscape is too subtle, too recondite, to yield to any simple search formula. And that is why dedicated explorers have a good chance of making unexpected discoveries in sinkholes, springs, mine faces, old and new excavations, and, best of all, throughout Florida's rivers and coastlines.

Florida also has two great geological virtues, at least from a paleontological viewpoint: mild-mannered tectonics and perennially wet depositional systems. These factors favor beautiful preservation of delicate and sometimes unusually complete fossil skeletons. No state, except Nebraska, has such a rich record of vertebrate fossils spanning the past 25 million years.

The true wealth of Florida's paleontological resources has been fully recognized only during the past two decades. As I see it, two fundamental factors drive this renaissance of Florida Paleontology: the Florida Museum of Natural History and the amateur community. These two institutions support each other and have developed a vital symbiotic relationship in Florida.

The rise of amateur involvement in Florida paleontology followed a parallel course. The *Plaster Jacket* publication began in 1965; annual meetings began in 1976; and the Florida Palentological Society was incorporated in 1978.

This symbiosis that I refer to can be measured in the impressive growth of the Florida Museum's fossil collections during the past two decades. That growth has stemmed directly from amateur involvement. In the mid-1960s Ben Waller began exploring diverse sites in the Santa Fe River, and when museum curators (Clayton Ray and I) showed an interest, he freely collaborated. A landmark of this early example of amateur-professional cooperation is the amazing discovery of "Big Bird," named *Titanis walleri*.

My own favorite example is the "Horned Wonder of the Bone Valley," an exceedingly rare animal discovered by Frank Garcia in the phosphate mines. Frank donated the skull, Howard Converse extensively repaired and restored it, and I described it as the new genus and species *Kyptoceras amatorum*. The species name can mean either "of the lovers" or "belonging to the amateurs."

I had already named a pronghorn antelope after Frank, so this was my opportunity to acknowledge the whole Florida amateur community. The powerful symbiosis between professionals and amateurs has brought Florida paleontology to its present high status. I am certain that the fossil wealth of this great state will continue to yield up its ancient secrets, slowly but surely, to this wonderful collaboration.

S. David Webb
Curator, Vertebrate Paleontology
Florida Museum of Natural History

Few disciplines encompassed by the study of nature and human culture have such wide appeal as those of paleontology and archaeology. Part of this interest comes from the fact that anyone may stumble across an exciting discovery.

For some, that's all it takes to spark an interest in becoming a serious amateur or, occasionally, to aspire to a professional career. It is the quests for knowledge about the animals and people who lived and died in different environments during times almost forgotten.

For the professionals it is the quest to decipher the preserved evidence of past environments, flora and fauna. For the amateurs it is the quest and the excitement of discovery, as well as an appreciation of scientific knowledge and their attachment to a favorite fossil or artifact for display and preservation.

Mark Renz's book, *Fossiling in Florida: A Guide for Diggers and Divers,* should serve to strengthen the bridge between the amateur and professional communities. Amateurs have found and will continue to find many sites in Florida, yet it is the scientific community that is accomplished in the proper identification and interpretation of significant finds.

Renz has assembled a friendly text from the standpoint of a serious, well-read amateur. His work promises to be an excellent educational guide for those interested in paleontology or seeking information about their fortuitous discovery of fossil remains. As a thoughtful, seasoned veteran, Renz can assist others who aspire to gain more knowledge about the topic outside the rigors of academia. He provides a framework for communicating, in lay terms, the basics of paleontology and the importance of the Florida resource.

Florida truly has an important and unusually well preserved assemblage of vertebrate fossil remains dating from several millions of years old to the termination of the last ice age, which ended a mere 10,000 years ago. Near the trail's end of this legacy the first humans (Paleo-Indians) came to Florida and coexisted among and hunted large Pleistocene animals the likes of which our species will never see again.

The bottom-line monetary worth of objects is often the time bandit of paleontology and archaeology. It has always been a balancing act to understand and control the excitement of initial discovery and to develop the skills needed to recognize significant finds. Finds such as the Leisey shell pit should and did have its day in the sunlight of scientific scrutiny. If the promotion of knowledge is the key to the salvation of the resource, the work of Mark Renz promises to provide a timely and much needed step forward.

Jim Dunbar, Archaeologist

Those who have tapped the rich fossil lodes of Florida have experienced the hardships, the puzzlements, and the triumphs that Mark Renz describes in this book. For those just beginning the hunt, this book will be an eye opener and a delight. No one writing about amateur paleontology in Florida has painted fossil hunting the way Mark has. He pursues the animals of Florida's rich biological past with the passion and wonderment of a true lover of life. As he writes, you can feel him striving to understand the life and death of millions of animals over millions of years.

Like most fossil finders, Mark sought answers to questions: What have I found? When did it live? What was Florida like when the animal was alive? He hunted information about ancient beasts with the same fervor that he hunted their fossilized remains. When he had absorbed all he could learn from local libraries, he took his quest to the professionals. As a diving participant in the nationally renowned Aucilla River Prehistory Project, Mark soaked up knowledge from paleontologists and archaeologists who are finding answers to the last chapter of Florida's fossil past: the great Pleistocene extinctions that occurred 12,000 years ago.

Mark has hunted in rock pits, on spoil piles, and along beaches. But his greatest finds have been in flowing water—fossils uncovered by the swirling erosion of streams and rivers. He sets aside fear and explores the murky depths of a river bottom hole because he knows that this is where the swift water slows and drops some of its burden. His search combines intellectual knowledge and uncanny intuition, and the combination rarely fails. In Mark's short career as avocational paleontologist, he has made outstanding finds.

In this book, Mark Renz tells it all. His practical "how to" suggestions about fossiling are invaluable. His storytelling is exciting. And through it all runs his wonderful love of life, present and past.

Robin Brown
Author, *Florida's Fossils* and *Florida's First People*

Preface

I am an amateur paleontologist, which means one who loves fossiling but chooses not to make it a profession. That definition seems odd to me given the number of people I encounter daily who are not very fond of their professions. Many work out of necessity, because they have created a life in which they must pay a lot of bills every month. But they don't really love what they do.

While I can't blame these people and have found myself in undesirable jobs over the years, I decided in 1995 that I was going to turn my love of paleontology into a profession. Not in academics or research or fieldwork, but as a guide who directs people to fossil locales. Once there, I would point out which fossils to look for, how to look for them, and how to work with the professional community so that science—and ultimately all of us—benefit.

As an "amateur professional," then, I am well aware that those who come with me to search in creeks and rivers carry with them a double-edged shovel. How we beginners pursue fossiling after our first outing will impact paleontology in a positive or negative way—depending on our individual attitudes about the subject. If we share our information and finds with members of the scientific community and allow them to interpret the data, we all benefit from a clearer picture of our fascinating past. If we hoard our secret spots and ancient treasures, keeping them only for ourselves or selling them to the highest commercial bidder, then crucial pieces of the paleontological puzzle may be forever lost.

This book is dedicated to everyone with an interest in paleontology (or the closely related field of archaeology), whether beginner or professional. We all had to start somewhere, and most of us are heading in the same direction, which is a positive one. Even if we don't always see eye to eye, our mutual goals will be more easily achieved if we can walk in each other's shoes for a time.

Acknowledgments

I owe considerable gratitude to the following people at the Florida Museum of Natural History: David Webb, Russ McCarty, Bruce MacFadden, Marc Franks, Karen Walker, and Gary Morgan (formerly with the museum). Each of them—especially Russ McCarty—has given either time or the museum's resources to help me complete this book.

A hearty thank you as well to Robin Brown for passing his passion for old bones on to me; to my brother Dave and the late Terry Hacker for leading me to the fossilized whale earbone that first piqued my interest; to Barbara Toomey for her constructive review of the manuscript in its early stages; to Barbara Oehlbeck for being an unending source of information and friendship; and to University Press of Florida editors Meredith Morris-Babb and Gillian Hillis along with freelance copyeditor Victoria Haire.

I would be remiss if I didn't thank Rob Neuhauser for his willingness to photograph various fossils before this book was even accepted, and Sunny Sung for volunteering to shoot most of the pictures for the Prehistoric Portraits section.

Most of my gratitude is reserved for my beautiful wife, Marisa, for her wonderful illustrations and whose patience, sweetness, and love go on and on and on. I never thought a honeymoon could last this long.

1

Help Wanted,
No Degree Necessary

On-the-Job Training Is the Only Way to Go

That chilly November morning in 1990, even the squirrels in Nashville appeared to be shivering as they descended a frost-shrouded tree in search of a buried meal. It would have been a great day for me to stay indoors.

Instead, I was tightening the bungie cords that secured most of my worldly possessions on the backseat of my 1200 cc un-American motorcycle. I karate-kicked my leg over the seat, pressed the electric starter, and listened as the huge engine purred softly. Tipping my helmet to my nutty friends, I pointed the front tire south. In minutes, I was following the asphalt trail leading to my old hometown of Fort Myers, Florida.

I had been home a few months when my brother Dave told me about a stretch of the Caloosahatchee River in Fort Myers, where he and a friend looked for shark teeth in the banks when the fish weren't biting—which was almost every time they were out.

To understand how the teeth got in the banks in the first place, you have to understand a little about the U.S. Army Corps of Engineers. Over the last hundred years, they have made a living out of straightening and deepening rivers. They're also known for their locks, which stop or speed up the flow of certain waterways. To some, the Corps' handiwork is a blessing, while to others it's a curse. To you, the fossil hunter, it's the opportunity to dive into the past without getting wet.

By definition, a fossil is the preserved remains or imprints of once living creatures. Minerals get deposited within tiny pores of the bone, and eventually even the bone substance itself. The bones or teeth do not lose their original shape, but they can be replaced atom for atom by such minerals as carbonates and silicates. The imprint of an animal's foot can also be classified as a fossil, or trace fossil as some call it, because it is still the representation of a once living animal.

Mako shark teeth. Photo by Rob Neuhauser.

Whale ear bone. Photo by
Rob Neuhauser.

All that dried-out river bottom, and all those corners the Corps cut
through to straighten out the zigs and zags of the old Caloosahatchee, were
piled onto the existing riverbanks. If you know where to sift through the
sand—not just in the Caloosahatchee, but in the banks of countless other
waterways they dredged as well—you may come away with enough fossils
to start your own mini-Smithsonian.

The place Dave took me to by boat was a spot we would later call "Old
Faithful" because it always produced a lot of shark teeth. While searching
for teeth, I became intrigued by what else kept turning up. Strangely
shaped bits of bone were present, many of which were too similar in design

Are these Native Ameri-
can beads or worm cast-
ings created in soft clay
eons ago? It depends on
whom you ask. Either
way, once they were cre-
ated, Native Americans
may have worn them as
beads. Photo by Rob
Neuhauser.

to be mere coincidence. What were they, and when were they a living part of some prehistoric creature?

I checked the public library and found a book called *Florida's Fossils* by an ear, nose, and throat doctor named Robin Brown. When I recognized that the things I had found were prehistoric whale ear bones, bear incisors, horse teeth, and alligator doo-doo, my adrenaline began pumping.

Soon I was making weekly treks to Old Faithful. Because I didn't have a boat and I couldn't expect my brother to drop everything and chauffeur me to the site, it became a real challenge to get there.

I remember one hot and humid Saturday morning I got the itch to go. I was so determined to poke around in those riverbanks that I hid my motorcycle in an orange grove on the south side of the river and swam over to the north side where the fossils were beckoning. I carried with me a small garden trowel, empty fossil bag, boat cushion for flotation, lunch, a jug of water, and a watch that I later discovered wasn't waterproof.

Halfway across the 300-foot span of river, a 60-foot yacht rounded a curve into my view, doing at least 15 knots. I considered my options, deciding that swimming like a madman seemed to be the most appropriate choice. I barely made it out of the vessel's way.

But before I could breathe a sigh of relief, white-capped waves, like those that pound the beaches of Southern California, broke away from the stern of the vessel in a long V pattern. With no experience or equipment for surfing, all I could do was hold onto my gear and breath as each wave slammed unmercifully into me.

I did well that day, uncovering a two-inch mako shark tooth, three horse teeth, a bison tooth, and a beautiful fragment of mammoth tooth. At dusk, when it was time to leave, I got about halfway across the river again when I noticed what appeared to be a used tractor tire floating slowly but steadily upriver near the shoreline. A closer inspection revealed that the tire was actually a 10-foot alligator beginning its weekly search for food.

I muttered a few profound and profane expressions, and once again considered my options, the first of which was to scream "Help!" at the top of my lungs. Wisely, I chose instead to keep my mouth shut. I stretched out on my back and slowly maneuvered downriver, being careful not to create any large ripples that might draw attention to myself. Fortunately, the gator's vision was as bad as my foresight.

I continued to work Old Faithful in 1991 and 1992, gradually breaking away to explore other parts of the river, either by walking along its banks or borrowing my brother's canoe. The more river I investigated, the more I realized that Old Faithful was not the only great fossil-hunting site in Florida. But it sure was a great beginning.

If in half a dozen short years someone who is as new to fossil hunting as I am can accumulate a few thousand prehistoric horse teeth, several thousand shark teeth, half of a 20-foot-tall giant ground sloth, a 12-foot ancient cousin to the manatee called a dugong, remains of jaguars, saber-toothed cats, mammoths, mastodons, giant armadillos, tortoises, tapirs, bison, and whales—anyone can do it. And you don't need a college degree.

If you're at all curious about the past, you'll find Florida is one of the easiest places in the world to peer into it. Hop into almost any creek or river (cautiously, of course), stroll along one of the state's hundreds of miles of beaches, or pick through a pile of sand left over from a phosphate- or limestone-and-gravel pit. You'll find the past right at your fingertips.

Whether they are shells (invertebrate fossils) or bones and teeth (vertebrate fossils), Florida's crust is full of them. All you need is a little planning, a little patience, a little perseverance, and a slight measure of luck. (I usually carry along a fossilized rabbit's foot.)

According to scientists, 95 percent of every type of plant and animal ever to live on Earth has yet to be discovered. In other words, only 5 percent of the total sum of life on Earth has been accounted for. So we amateurs have countless opportunities to discover something new—or rather, something old that's new.

Most professional paleontologists (who study ancient animals and plants) and archaeologists (who study ancient humans and their cultures)

Cow shark tooth. Photo by Rob Neuhauser.

Widening the Caloosahatchee River in 1965 by the U.S. Army Corps of Engineers. Photos by Robin Brown.

are too busy in labs assembling bones and analyzing data from fossils already collected to spend more than one month per year searching for anything new. For every day in the field, about 10 days are needed to conserve, curate, study, then publish.

That means the amateur has a realistic chance to stumble upon a major missing link between a sea creature and land animal; or to determine when a certain animal began to develop wings or lose them; or to close in on a more precise date or reason so many large animals became extinct at the end of the last ice age, and where humans fit into the picture.

You and I can be the scientists' eyes in the field. What an honor it would be to discover an animal that in some way added to the whole of life's existence. Even if we didn't come across something new, wouldn't it be grand to actually see firsthand what we've read about all these years in magazines and books? We get the chance every time we go fossil hunting in Florida.

One of the pioneers in paleontology, the late George Gaylord Simpson, described vividly how fossil hunting differs from other passionate avocations or professions in his book *Fossils and the History of Life:*

> Fossil hunting is far the most fascinating of all sports. It has some danger, enough to give it zest and probably about as much as in the average modern engineered big-game hunt, and the danger is wholly to the hunter. It has uncertainty and excitement, and all the thrills of gambling with none of its vicious qualities. The hunter never knows what his bag may be, perhaps nothing, perhaps a creature never before seen by human eyes.
>
> It requires knowledge, skill, and some degree of hardihood. And its results are so much more important, more worthwhile, and more enduring than those of any other sport. The fossil hunter does not kill: he resurrects. And the result of this sport is to add to the sum of human pleasure and to the treasures of human knowledge.

Enough said. Let's start the hunt.

2

It's All a State of Mind

An Interview with Florida

If Florida could talk about its past, here's what it might have to say:

I wasn't always in this shape. Why, if you had known me when I was 50 million years younger, you'd be surprised at how much weight I've gained, lost, gained, and lost again.

My parents, North America and Africa, met during a continental collision about 210 million years ago. It was a strange marriage, made even stranger by the fact that they were separated at the time.

I take after my mother, Africa, the most, in that my roots began there. When the two of them slowly collided and then moved apart, a small portion of Africa was left behind to become part of Florida and a few other southeastern states.

I grew gradually under the ocean's surface for about 160 million years. You wouldn't believe the changes that took place over that short geologic span of time. When I was born, dinosaurs were still in their infancy. Mam-

Dark area indicates size of ancient Florida's land mass during different ice ages. Broken line on far right illustration indicates when the state was much wider than today.

mals were also around, although they were small, shrewlike creatures that lived pretty much in the shadows of dinosaurs.

By the time I really began to develop as an above-water landmass 37 million years ago, dinosaurs had been extinct for nearly 30 million years. That's why no one has ever found their fossilized remains here. I wasn't much to look at, starting out as a series of dotted islands over much of what is now northern and central Florida.

My life has been influenced heavily by multiple glacial cycles. Throughout my childhood, and even now as a young adult, ice gathering at Earth's two poles has caused my borders to swell tremendously, then shrink again as the ice melted. Even as recently as 12,000 years ago, my west coast alone extended another 60 to 75 miles into the Gulf of Mexico.

As ice underwent this melting process, it gradually flooded my boundaries to today's current levels. At times, however, the water rose to cover all but a 100-mile strip of land running north to south, with less than 10 miles exposed east to west.

Between each glacial cycle there were different types of animals traipsing around on my soil or swimming within my shallow seas. Their fossilized remains are often found mixed together, even though they may have lived and died millions of years apart. That's because the constant pounding of ocean waves has tossed and turned my sandy bottom until it's sometimes difficult to tell precisely where—or when—many of my creatures lived or died.

Some of these animals were spared the force of water and were preserved in shallow graves a few feet below my swamps, creeks, or rivers. Because I was not rocked by any major geologic upheavals such as earthquakes or volcanoes, these expired animals survived the hands of time undisturbed in my underground safety deposit boxes.

That is, until my creeks and rivers cut deep grooves through my surface, washing some fossils out while burying others. Or when land developers broke in while replacing my natural beauty with concrete condos and well-manicured golf courses. Or when you, the fossil hunter, come along to resurrect the past with your thirst for knowledge.

Welcome to my world. I hope you enjoy it, learn from it, respect it, and leave it a little cleaner than the way you found it.

3

Even Hindsight Isn't 20/20

Charting Florida's Sometimes Confusing Past

Note: "Millions of years ago" is expressed as Ma. B.P. means "Before Present" when discussing the late Pleistocene and Holocene epochs.

As the state of Florida disclosed in the last chapter, it was an underwater shelf on the African continent until a collision with North America about 200 Ma left it at our country's doorstep. While elsewhere dinosaurs were consuming anything and everything in their paths and melting glaciers with their resulting flatulence, Florida remained underwater—holding its breath.

By 65 Ma, most of the larger dinosaurs were gone. Five million years later, the state's shallow seas began to develop a limestone floor. Because the material was so new geologically, you won't find any Paleozoic trilobites or Mesozoic ammonites in Florida today. Nor will you find any trace of the dinosaurs.

MARISA '95

In fact, it was only in the last 37 million years that Florida began to emerge from the sea to support any land animals. With dinosaurs gone, mammals thrived. In the last three and a half million years, hominids crawled onto the landscape. They created language, which meant scientists had an excuse to use words that dilated the pupils of the listener. One of those words was Cenozoic, an era broken down into two shorter periods and seven even briefer epochs. Each epoch rhymes and can legally be used in close games of Scrabble. They are:

Paleocene—65 to 56.5 Ma. Not much is known about these years, except that mammals occupying higher ground in other states increased in size and numbers. Some of them adapted "sea legs" and took to the ocean. Others developed wings.

Eocene—56.5 to 35.5 Ma. Florida's limestone floor began to take shape, consisting of skeletons of tiny organisms known as foraminifera. Shells, corals, and college spring breakers joined the party. Once compacted, they became calcium carbonate stone. Covering the floor were sand dollars and sea urchins. Sharks, 65-foot-long snakelike whales called archaeocete, sea

Limestone karst, Hamilton County. Photo by Robin Brown.

cows, sea turtles, and sea snakes (primitive politicians) also inhabited the waters. Fossilized teeth from Archaeocete and Eocene sharks can be found in north and north-central Florida, as well as the panhandle.

Oligocene—35.5 to 23.3 Ma. Temperatures dropped in the North, and land emerged in the South, beginning first as a series of islands. Whales disappeared completely for the time being, sea cows were few and far between, and new groups of sharks moved in to apply for an occupational license.

As land bridges were formed by soil washing down from the continental landmass, and sand and shell fragments were laid down by ocean currents, above-water creatures began to retire and move into Florida. But these geologic changes were not steady. Over thousands and hundreds of thousands of years, the oceans would rise, drop, rise, and drop again.

Miocene—23.3 to 5.2 Ma. Although the land continued to bob up and down through different glacial cycles, it rose more than it dropped. At times, the state was slightly longer and twice its current width. Other times, it was less than 100 miles long and 10 miles wide.

North America and Eurasia got to know each other a little better during this epoch because of an exchange program known as the Bering Strait Land Bridge. This allowed mammals from both continents to intersperse and widen their territories. Mammals eventually moved southeast, with many species winding up in Florida for the same reason we humans move here today—a warm climate and a chance to escape a state income tax.

In the ocean, rays, sea cows, bony fish, dolphins, sharks, and other creatures were plentiful. One shark, known today as the extinct giant white, may have grown to 60 feet in length, with massive seven-inch teeth. It would have easily taken the bite out of the great white starring in the movie *Jaws*. The extinct giant white ranged as far south as Naples along Florida's west coast, and as far north as the Carolinas.

Land animals, such as bone-crushing dogs, huge ground sloths, rhinoceroses, saber-toothed cats, three-toed collie-sized horses, tapirs, and deer, also flourished. Many of these animals made their way to the southernmost tip of Florida (and beyond, since the state was at times larger).

Reptiles included a land tortoise with a five-foot-long shell, a crocodile that exceeded 30 feet in length, iguanas, and gila monsters. Florida's sky in the Miocene was a busy place as well. Bats, hawks, osprey, cormorants, turkeys, and vultures with wing spans of 15 feet became residents.

Pliocene—5.2 to 1.81 Ma. A lot of glacial activity took place during this epoch with temperatures dropping worldwide. At least a half dozen times, sea levels rose anywhere from 15 to 20 feet above today's level, then dropped some 300 feet as temperatures soared again. The lower sea levels meant Florida's landmass increased to twice today's width.

The drop in sea levels also created a wide savanna along the state's western coastline connecting to the Caribbean coast of Mexico and Yucatan, then on to South America. This land corridor, called the Great American Faunal Interchange, opened up a path for wildlife migrations north and south.

'98 Marisa R.

Dugongs (manatee cousins) and long-beaked dolphins died out here and were replaced by the gentle, slow-moving manatees that today are bordering on extinction. Baleen whales evolved into their current enormous size, and crocodiles disappeared until recent times.

Pleistocene—1.81 Ma to 10,000 years BP. (This time is not rigidly defined by geologists.) Sea levels continued to rise and fall at least two dozen times. A large number of strange and wondrous mammals drifted into Florida during the Pleistocene.

A carnivorous bird called *Titanis walleri* stood 6 to 10 feet tall and may have run down three-toed horses for its meals. If this feathery giant could have spoken, scientists believe its first words might have been "Here Kitty, Kitty!"

Horses, deer, peccaries (a pig-size rodent), five-foot beavers, and pseudo-camels thrived here. Sloths far bigger than their predecessors (or the small three-toed tree sloths of South America today) traveled from

South America to Florida. The largest, *Eremotherium*, reached 20 feet from head to tail and weighed as much as five tons.

Armadillos were also considerably larger than those that so often wind up as roadkill today. One, called *Glyptotherium*, was about the size of an economy car and weighed as much as 10 professional football players. Texans are thought to have their roots in this epoch.

Although some elephantlike proboscidians existed in Florida prior to the Pliocene and Pleistocene, mammoths were the most common over the last five million years. Bison were also prolific.

Holocene—10,000 years BP to present. The wilds of Florida are pretty tame compared with the Florida of 10,000 years ago. What happened to the mighty mammoth and the giant ground sloth? Where can you find a saber-toothed cat today? Creatures that took millions of years to evolve disappeared mysteriously at the beginning of the Holocene.

Another mass extinction had occurred at the end of the Miocene five million years ago, when at least 60 genre of land animals disappeared from North America. In both cases, sudden climatic changes may have caused many of the losses. Climates were either too hot or too cold, there may have been too much water or not enough, or the oxygen supply was diminished.

However, humans may have played a dramatic role in bringing about animal extinctions at the end of the Pleistocene. Although we have slowly evolved over the last three and a half million years, we were absent from the state until 10,000 to 15,000 years BP. Some of our ancestors were here to see, if not participate in, the demise of many of these creatures.

And the losses are still adding up. Manatees, Key deer, wood rats, black bears, Florida panthers, and rational-minded people are just a few on their way out.

4

Which Came First, the Fossilized Chicken or the Egg?

Whether you lean toward evolution or creation, the unfolding drama of life is remarkable.

From a religious perspective, many view the past as a series of organized perfections with a grand scheme in mind. A divine being constructs a planet, throws in some darkness and light, sprinkles the basics of life upon it, and then overnight creates men and women to act as caretakers of the whole affair.

Through the Coke bottle–thick eyeglasses of some scientists, life might be viewed as a series of trials and errors, with no easily understood end goal in mind. Things came to be what they are by different forms of energy constantly coming in contact with each other in various contexts. They bounced off or melded together until something clicked, something that became compatible (at least temporarily), that eventually added up to what appears to be a well-orchestrated end result.

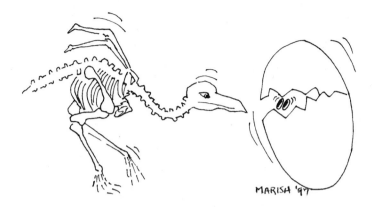

MARISH '97

Who knows? Perhaps even that scenario is the master plan some supreme being had in mind. From my experiences, no one among us has a tight enough grip on reality to say with absolute certainty how things truly came to be. So I prefer to consider every explanation as conceivable whether it's based on theory, fact, or faith. I must admit, though, that some explanations seem far more conceivable than others.

Personally, it doesn't matter to me if some God snapped his or her fingers and in milliseconds effected major changes on Earth or throughout the cosmos. Nor does it matter that life may have evolved more slowly, over hundreds, thousands, millions, billions, trillions of years or more. It's still fascinating to collect fossils and from them, to note how certain animals (including humans) have changed over whatever period of time they may have lived.

Consider the generally accepted story of the 58- to 30-million-year-old horse. Originally, this knee-high mammal had four toes on its stubby front legs and three on the hind legs. It was built perfectly for darting around in the thick forests that covered much of North America at the time.

But as the forests later evolved into open grasslands, the horse changed too, gradually losing some of its toes and becoming a longer-legged, faster-running animal that could escape its prey on the open plains.

Then there was the steppe mammoth of Eurasia, which managed to adjust to a several-hundred-thousand-year transition from a warm climate to a cold one. It developed smaller ears and longer hair to keep warm, and longer tusks to scrape through snow for food. As its diet changed, so did the chewing surface of the mammoth's teeth—from eight to 10 enamel plates to twice that number.

Miniature mammoths were another marvel of adaptation. Their fossilized remains have been found in such places as California's Channel Islands, Malta and Sicily, the rugged coast of Wrangel Island in the Arctic Ocean off northeastern Siberia, and Timor in the South Pacific. Each time mammoths were trapped on an island by rising seas of the Pleistocene, they became miniaturized.

In Malta and Sicily, during a brief time 500,000 years ago when the two were joined together as one island, these dwarf proboscideans were only three feet high. The six-foot mammoths of Wrangel Island may have died out as recently as 7,000 years ago. Yet older, larger mammoth remains were discovered in the same area dating back 12,000 years, which leads scientists to believe it took only 5,000 years for them to shrink.

What caused the change? Most researchers think Wrangel and other islands didn't produce enough food to support growing numbers of mammoths. There was also an absence of predators. If the mammoths failed to adapt to an island's limited food supply, they were bound for rapid extinction. Eventually, such was the fate of even the dwarf mammoths.

Another explanation is that there may have been two types of mammoths occupying the islands at the same time, and the larger ones gradu-

A Quick Lesson in Classification

The Swedish naturalist Linnaeus (1707–1778) came up with a simple way to fit animals into organized categories. Here is the classification, as it is called, of the modern horse:

Kingdom—Animalia

Phylum—Chordata

Subphylum—Vertebrata (includes fish, amphibians, reptiles, birds, mammals)

Class—Mammalia

Order—Perissodactyla (joins other odd-toed ungulates, including tapirs, rhinos, and some extinct groups)

Family—Equidae (includes all fossils and living horses, zebras, asses, and their relatives)

Genus—*Equus L.*

Species—*caballus*

ally died out or swam off the islands to search for more food. Elephants today think nothing of taking long swims in the ocean, even though they're occasionally attacked by sharks. They love the water. It's entirely possible that mammoths could have swum 25 miles or more to some island and settled there until their food supply dwindled.

In support of a larger mammoth reducing the size of its bone structure to survive in a limited food environment, consider the modern Key deer. As a variation of white-tailed deer, this two-foot-high herbivore lives on islands known as the Florida Keys. North of the Keys, Florida white-tailed deer are also smaller than their northern counterparts since the lack of cold weather means they have no need to store up a lot of body fat.

While larger mammals may have shrunk on islands, smaller mammals like rodents may have actually increased in size, because there were fewer predators for them to dodge. Also, without predators, rodents may have grown in size to compete for mates.

Reptiles, such as alligators and turtles, have had to adapt over time as well, and have done an even greater job of it than many mammals. Existing for over 150 million years, they have managed to survive whatever forces of nature wiped out dinosaurs 65 Ma. and two other major extinctions leading up to today.

Even in one generation, an alligator can go to extremes to survive. In the wild, alligators generally grow about a foot a year until they reach an age of eight or nine years old. In captivity, they can be fed a high-protein diet and grow as much as three feet a year. If need be, they can also stunt their growth to adjust to their environment. I once saw a 10-year-old that had spent its entire life confined to a two-foot-long aquarium. The alligator had grown no larger than its home.

5

A Day in the Life of
a Giant Ground Sloth

She was on her last legs. Old and suffering from acute arthritis, she felt pain with every movement of her tired and worn-out body. She had five tons to support, 20 feet of enormous bulk. Each day she had to consume several hundred pounds of greenery if she was to survive.

Even though her kind was larger than any other land animal ever to live in Florida, nature was no less cruel. Saber-toothed cats, a third again the size of a modern African lion, occasionally hunted in packs. Like many predators, they went first for the sick and weak. She had to keep up her strength, or she would quickly become the easiest of prey.

When the peninsula's subtropical sun was directly overhead, she was overcome with thirst. So she made her way feebly to a nearby slough. Water was her lifeblood, and a creature her size required copious amounts. She lapped up the cool, clear liquid until she had her fill, then turned toward

dry ground. But her feet wouldn't budge. Her tremendous weight had buried them in the soft muck of the slough.

She tried desperately to free herself but didn't have the energy. After numerous attempts, she collapsed in a heap and lay still, breathing heavily. When night fell, she was still slumped over, her will to survive rapidly waning.

Two days later, several hungry saber-toothed cats paced back and forth anxiously at the slough's edge. Vulturelike birds circled high overhead. An alligator floated motionless nearby, as if sensing it was almost time.

A million years passed.

In December of 1992, I was exploring a southwest Florida stream with a mask and snorkel, searching for fossils. To me, nothing compares to our creeks and rivers, especially those that are shallow enough to snorkel. In the southwestern part of the state where I live, these caramel-colored waterways contain some of the most interesting fossils to be found anywhere.

The creeks and rivers themselves offer unparalleled beauty. Their banks are often 15 to 20 feet high and lined with solid oaks, old-growth bald cypress trees, and sky-reaching sabal palmetto palms. They so resemble eras gone by that I half expect to come face-to-face with a proud Paleoindian or a ferocious saber-toothed cat.

There are approximately 14 creeks and three rivers in Lee County alone. I have ventured into most of them and have found fossils in all but one. With 67 counties in the state and a good possibility that there are a tremendous amount of fossils in most of the creeks and rivers in those counties as well . . . do you get the picture? Florida has a heck of a lot of fossils.

The way I figure it, if a lanky amateur like me can find numerous ancient bones and teeth, anyone can. But that doesn't mean it's always easy. Locating the good stuff is a mixture of skill, luck, and persistence. In 95 degree heat, I've had to hike several miles up or down creeks, in the water, along their banks, through thorns and thick saw palmetto shrubs, and over and under barbed wire fences (being careful to get permission from the landowner first). All this while wearing a steaming-hot wetsuit and carrying food and water, mask and snorkel, as well as a fossil net (which, I hope, is full of bones on the return trip).

Overall, the spoils have been well worth the hardships. For instance, one creek—which I have become intimately familiar with and which has been responsible for my sweating off countless pounds of fat—almost always gives up wonderful finds. There are pockets of fossils every half mile or so that are so rich they appear to have been dumped there by the truckload.

On my first day in this particular creek, in an area about the size of an average living room, I uncovered 44 horse teeth, seven glyptodont (car-size armadillo) scutes, eight mako shark teeth about two inches long, 25 alligator teeth, umpteen turtle and tortoise shell fragments, four whale vertebrae, two whale teeth, 12 deer antler fragments, seven barracuda teeth, six snaggletooth shark teeth, three great white teeth, four whale inner earbones, garfish scales, and various other fossils.

I have had other equally rewarding days in the same creek. However, none have been quite as exciting for me as the day I trudged about two miles up a portion of the creek I had never searched before. I had started out at 8:00 A.M., and it was now pushing dusk. Trees along the bank were casting long shadows over the water, making visibility difficult. When I finished, I would still have to make a two-mile trek back to the car.

I was frustrated because I hadn't found anything, not even a modern turtle shell fragment. After traveling nearly a quarter of a mile farther, I was just about ready to throw in the towel for another day when I noticed a few small bone fragments in about two feet of water just downstream from a bend. I donned my mask, lay down in the creek, and began inching my way upstream.

After several feet the bone fragments increased in number and size. Still, I couldn't identify any of them. They were too badly splintered. Then, off to my left a few feet, my peripheral vision picked up a large black object sticking out of the sand. Accustomed to coming across submerged tree trunks, I casually scraped the object with my fingernail. But this time, instead of sinking into soft, water-logged wood, my nails met with resistance.

Having been fooled many times into thinking I had found a large bone that turned out to be wood or metal, I still didn't get excited. In fact, I was feeling a little irritated that I wasn't able to confirm my suspicions immediately. Halfheartedly, I dug out around the object and before long had it freed from its watery grave. It was only then that I realized I had half of what appeared to be a massive leg bone. Was it from a mammoth? A mastodon?

To date, it was my largest find, and the adrenaline surged through my body. I stuck my hand through the sand where I had found the bone and felt something else hard that my fingernails couldn't gouge. When I worked it out and held it up, I knew right away what I had found. In my hand was a claw core, or toenail, over a foot long. It belonged to an *Eremotherium*, the largest of the sloths and the biggest type of land animal ever to live in Florida.

I came up out of the water screaming like a passionate lover, "Yes! Yes! Yes!"

There were more bones buried in the sand, but it was getting too dark to make out anything. I hated to leave, but the search would have to wait until the following morning.

That night, I slept with the claw next to my pillow. Every time I would half wake up and realize what I had found, I had to touch it to make sure I hadn't dreamed the whole thing.

I arrived at daybreak, blowing the sand away with my hands in about two feet of water. Everywhere I looked there were large black chunks of fossilized bone. By the time the day ended, I had found several hundred pounds of the animal—not articulated, or joined together—but scattered in every direction. Had it been articulated, the wisest thing to do would have been to call the Florida Museum of Natural History in Gainesville to ask for guidance in removing it.

There were two claw cores, one about 15 inches and the other 16 inches long. A section of the jaw was uncovered with three teeth still in place, plus there were other entire teeth and partials. Seventeen vertebrae would eventually come out, as well as both astragalus (ankle bones) as large as bowling balls, three toe or finger bones, the snout bone, and two tibias (shin bones; one about 26 inches long and 17 inches wide at the upper end).

Later, a third partial tibia was found, indicating there may have been more than one sloth at the site.

These bones, along with the remains of a different, smaller species I found nearby, got me to thinking. Was this a place sloths came to die of old age or when they were sick? Was there an environmental catastrophe that brought on their deaths, such as a major drought or extreme cold weather? Did they simply die from a lack of vegetation? Was there a flash flood that killed them? Or were humans somehow involved?

Near as I could determine by examining the bones, humans hadn't killed these animals. In fact, a more likely scenario was that if the sloth was a sociable animal, a lot of them lived in this area, and hence they would die in the same general spot.

And the sloth wasn't the only animal to have been here. Scattered under and around the bones were a number of alligator teeth. Were they lost feeding on the carcass? Did they kill the sloth? Or were the teeth from a completely different time period and just happened to wash into the site?

Beneath the sand, which was three feet deep in some places, the bones had been resting on a bottom that was a mixture of blue-green clay and ancient saltwater shells. Perhaps it was a shallow bay when the sloths died, and a nearby river delivered their bloated carcasses to this spot, where they gradually sank. Judging by the healthy-looking sabal palmetto trees that appeared to have been uprooted and washed into the creek by the previous rainy season's high water, the bones hadn't been exposed for long.

I consulted with veteran slother Don Serbousek in Daytona. He believed the large claws belonged to an animal perhaps 20 feet from head to tail. A sloth he found and contributed to the Daytona Museum of Arts and Sciences is approximately 14 feet, but its largest claw core is only eight inches.

Tracking Sloths in Florida

Florida's first sloths most likely arrived here in the late Miocene, at least eight or nine Ma, via the Central American mainland. The new arrivals were *Pliometanastes* and *Thinobadistes,* ancestors to later Pleistocene sloths. This theory of migration gained credibility when Dr. S. David Webb, curator of vertebrate fossils for the Florida Museum of Natural History, described *Meizonyx,* a new genus of large sloth, closely related to *Pliometanastes,* from the late Pliocene of El Salvador.

By the Pliocene, a ground sloth called *Glossotherium,* which resembled a 10- to 12-foot grizzly bear with a tail, had moved into Florida from South America. Then, in the Pleistocene, came *Eremotherium,* the largest land animal ever to set foot in Florida. This giant ground sloth grew in excess of 20 feet from head to tail, with a reach of another seven or eight feet.

Sloths are grouped with other edentates from South America, which include armadillos and glyptodonts (a car-size armadillolike animal). Edentate means "without teeth," which may have been true initially of some edentates, but evolution didn't sit still. The sloth eventually developed teeth, which lacked enamel, however.

Sloths were browsers, pulling down tree branches with their long-reaching arms to dine on the tender leaves.

Could Sloths Swim?

Yes, if you ask paleontologists Christian de Muizon, director of the French Institute of Andean Studies in Lima, Peru, and Greg McDonald of

Hagerman Fossil Beds National Monument in Idaho. (McDonald was a student at the University of Florida and did his master's thesis on North American *Megalonyx*.)

According to *Pacific Discovery* magazine on the Internet, the two men found a new genus and species of sloth in the coastal Peruvian desert that they believe was able to swim quite well.

Thalassocnus natans lived between 10 and 4 Ma. Its fossilized remains, which outnumbered the bones of marine mammals, were found in an area that used to be a shallow bay. Among the sloth's peculiarities were a premaxilla (bone at the front of the upper jaw) that was shaped like a manatee's.

The tibia (shin bone) was also almost as long as the femur (thigh bone), whereas in other sloths, the tibia is considerably smaller. Even the insertion points for the limb muscles and tail vertebrae suggested it was a swimmer rather than a freestanding diner.

The nearest relative of the Peruvian marine sloth in Florida is *Nothrotheriops,* which is very rare this side of New Mexico and the Grand Canyon, but common at Leisey shell pit in Ruskin, Florida.

Bigfoot of the Amazon

For years there have been a lot of rumors circulating in the Florida Everglades about a foul-smelling, hairy creature standing seven feet tall. Lee Krystek of the Museum of Unnatural History on the World Wide Web claims that South America, too, has had its share of sightings, although their strange creature with reddish hair is thought to be a 500-pound giant ground sloth.

Natives say this creature can make a skunk smell good, has a stare that will freeze you in your tracks, and is unaffected by spears and shotgun pellets.

By all accounts, ground sloths should have become extinct in Amazonia 8,700 years ago. But Argentinean explorer Ramon Lista claims he shot one and the animal was unfazed by the bullets. Gold miners also claim to have killed a giant ground sloth, yet no one ever came forward with a carcass.

Stories passed down by Indians in the Patagonia region describe giant ground sloths that slept away the days in burrows dug by their massive claws and came out to feed at night. Arrows had little effect against the beasts' hide.

An Argentine paleontologist in the early 1900s, Florentino Ameghino, obtained a portion of a sloth's hide found by a rancher in 1895. He noticed that small calcium nodules lined the hide, which would be ideal as an armor from predators. Ameghino explored the rancher's cave and others, finding more hides and fresh dung. He was so sure he had found a new creature that he named it after Lista: *Nemoylodon listai.*

It wasn't until the development of carbon-14 dating methods later in the twentieth century that the issue was put to rest. The dung was 10,000 years old, and the skin 5,000 years. The conditions in the cave acted as a preservative, causing the remains to appear fresh.

No giant sloth has yet to turn up in Amazonia, and so far no one has caught a skunkape in the Everglades.

Modern Sloth Facts

A sloth is called a sloth because it m . . . o . . . v . . . e . . . s . . . . . . s . . . o . . . . . . s . . . l . . . o . . . w.

Because sloths move so slowly, predators such as jaguars and harpy eagles have trouble spotting them.

There are seven types of modern sloths; five have three toes on each foot, and two have just two toes. All are found only in the jungles of Central and South America.

Three-toed sloths spend almost all of their lives in trees, coming down to the forest floor only once a week to defecate at the base of the tree.

Natives choose not to hunt sloths because they do not fall to the ground when wounded or killed. Instead, their claws continue to cling to the branches.

Despite their reputation for slowness, sloths can use their claws as weapons with considerable speed and skill.

Without a tree to cling to, today's sloths are helpless on the ground, unable to stand or walk. Their claws then become useful for pulling their bodies behind them.

Modern sloths are excellent swimmers.

Their hair reflects rain, but the continuous dampness causes green algae to grow in it. Moths lay eggs in the hair, and the caterpillars feed on the algae.

Motto of the Sloth
Don't pity me now,
don't pity me never
I'm going to do nothing
for ever and ever
JAMES AGATE, BRITISH DRAMA CRITIC

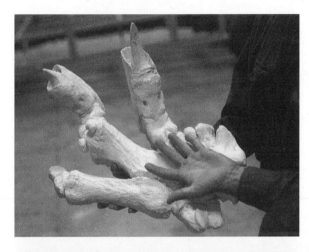

Cast of actual *Eremotherium* hand created by Don Serbousek of Ormond Beach, Fla. Photo by author.

Eremotherium nostril cavity. Photo by author.

Eremotherium humerus. Photo by author.

Eremotherium vertebra process. Photo by author.

Artist Marisa Renz with her oil painting of the *Eremotherium* to scale. Photo by author.

Eremotherium tooth. Photo by author.

Eremotherium metapodial (hand or foot bone). Photo by author.

Author holding two of the *Eremotherium* tibias. Three were found, indicating there was more than one sloth at the site. Photo by Marisa Renz.

Seventeen of the *Eremotherium* vertebrae. Photo by author.

Eremotherium metapodials (hand or foot bones). Photo by author.

Eremotherium jaw section with seven-inch teeth intact. Sloths were vegetarians. Photo by author.

Eremotherium inner claw cores. The two smaller ones belong to the author, while the large one is a cast of a Leisey shell pit claw belonging to Frank Garcia. Photo by author.

Florida's Fossil Sharks

A Brief Bite in Time

What Gulf-front chamber of commerce in its right mind would brag that its waters were inhabited by giant white sharks, and then invite the world to take a swim?

The Venice Area Chamber would, and the organization is very much in its right mind. That's because Venice Beach's 60-foot sharks became extinct five Ma. Today, only their fossilized teeth, and those of the giant white's smaller relatives, wash up on the beach.

Until recently, small teeth were so common at Venice's beaches that if you plunged your hands into the dark, coarse sand just below the shallow surf, chances are you would come up with at least one toothy specimen. And though Venice continues to live up to its reputation as the shark tooth capital of the world, many of its larger jewels are offshore, where only divers and hearty snorkelers can pluck them from their Gulf treasure chest.

Venice, like many coastal communities, was losing its sandy beaches to the relentless pounding of the ocean surf. So it was renourished with fresh sand—not taken from fossiliferous sources. Completed in 1996, the beach renourishment project added 1.2 million cubic yards of sand along a 19-mile stretch of the Gulf of Mexico. Teeth can still be found washed up on its beaches, but not as abundantly as before. Even with fewer teeth turning up, the Venice area has some grand beaches for the novice fossil hunter.

Why did Venice have so many live sharks in prehistoric times and not now? Nobody knows for sure. Perhaps cold water from previous ice ages drove sharks here to feed, breed, and die off Venice's subtropic coast. Or maybe they were attracted to the ancient large coral reef to the west of Venice, where they could dine on the fish.

If you visit the eight-mile stretch of sand that makes up Venice Municipal Beach, Golden Beach, and Caspersen Beach, don't leave until you have waded into the water with a "Florida snow shovel" (a square screen scoop

Possible shark bite marks on baleen whale rib found in the Orange River in Lee County. Photo by author.

Mammoth tooth, mammoth leg bone, horse tooth and ankle bone encrusted in barnacles, found by divers offshore from Venice Beach. It's not uncommon to find land animal remains offshore because in earlier times Florida's coastline was twice as wide as it is today. Photos by author.

on a long handle) and dragged the sea bottom for the remains of such ancient sharks as the dusky, bull, tiger, mako, sand, snaggletooth, and the big gal herself, "Meg," the extinct giant white.

It's best to search at low tide or after a storm. Look for shark tooth shapes in black, brown, red, or yellow. Wade into the water and drag your Florida snow shovel through any areas rich in black, pebbly material. The larger black chunks may be fossilized bone, such as sea cow rib sections and vertebrae, whale inner ear bones, eagle ray teeth and tail spines, fish mouth parts, turtle and giant tortoise shell fragments, or alligator teeth and bony armor.

Or uncover the teeth and bones of erstwhile land animals (remember, the state was twice as wide as today on numerous occasions): camels, three-toed horses, bison, sloths, giant armadillos, rhinoceros, and tapirs.

You may be able to buy a Florida snow shovel at the Circle K on the beach for about $14.95. You'll also need a container for your specimens, sunscreen, and sunglasses. There are restrooms and showers at Venice Municipal and Caspersen beaches. A lifeguard is on duty all day, every day at the municipal beach.

Venice Shark Tooth and Seafood Festival

Every year in August, the Venice Area Chamber of Commerce is host to a shark tooth festival in which thousands of people show up to buy or just view shark teeth and other fossils. Call (800) 940-SHAR(K).

To get there: Venice is 75 miles south of Tampa and 200 miles northwest of Miami, on Florida's southwest coast. Take Interstate 75 to exit 35, turn left onto Jacaranda Boulevard, then right at Venice Avenue, which will lead you directly to the beach. You can write the Venice Area Chamber of Commerce at 257 Tamiami Trail North 34285–1908, or call (941) 488-2236.

If you stop by the chamber, don't be surprised if someone gives your children a free bag of fossilized chompers. Venice is like that.

In the Beginning . . .

The earliest fossil record of the 344 shark species today comprises minute scales and teeth found in rocks dating to the late Silurian and early Devonian periods some 400 Ma. Because sharks have no skeleton, it's difficult to analyze shapes of braincases or fin structures. Fins are rarely preserved, and complete fossil sharks are seldom found.

In one discovery, entire shark carcasses were preserved in a bacteria-free environment in Upper Devonian Cleveland shales. Even muscle and kidney tissue could be examined in the rock.

Overall, the transition from species to species is not easy to trace. There are several theories as to the origins of sharks. One is that different cartilaginous fish (a group that includes sharks, rays, skates, and chimeras)

Cast of a seven-inch giant white *Carcharocles megalodon* tooth found in a North Carolina mine. Some researchers believe this is an ancestor of *Carcharodon*; others believe it is a variation of the same shark. Photo by author.

evolved from placoderms (now-extinct, bony-plated jawed fish). Or that placoderms and cartilaginous fish may have had a common ancestor. Still another theory is that the cartilaginous fish and a group of primitive jawless fish, such as thelodonts, both had a common ancestor.

Florida Sharks

During the Eocene epoch beginning 56.5 Ma and stretching forward to 35.5 Ma, sharks were busy leaving a fossil record. Among them were *Carcharodon auriculatus* (an extinct giant white), *Otodus obliquus* (extinct mackerel), and *Odontaspis microta*. Florida was under water for most of this epoch.

During the Oligocene 35.5 to 23.3 Ma, a new group was introduced: *Negaprion brevirostris* (lemon), *Hemipristis serra* (extinct snaggletooth), *Rhizoprionodon terrae-novae* (sharp-nose), and *Galeocerdo aduncas* (extinct tiger). Florida began to slowly emerge from the sea as an above-water landmass at the beginning of this epoch. It would rise and fall, then rise and fall even lower—exposing more land.

Carcharodon megalodon (another extinct giant white) bullied its way into Florida's waters during the mid-Miocene about 15 Ma and was gone by the end of the epoch. Others to become extinct in Florida waters (some are still alive elsewhere) are the *Isurus hastalis* (large mako), *Hemipristis serra* (extinct snaggletooth), and *Odontaspis cuspidata* (sand). Although sea levels rose and fell throughout this epoch, they dropped more than they rose, exposing even more land.

From the beginning to the end of the Pliocene 5.2 Ma to 1.81 Ma, and through the Pleistocene (1.81 Ma to 10,000 B.P.), Florida was covered and uncovered by seas. So when you find any of the shark teeth shown in this book, it is difficult to tell just from looking at the tooth exactly when in a particular epoch it was lost. For example, you may find two dusky shark teeth together; although they were lost by two different sharks over a hundred thousand years apart, they got mixed in with each other over time.

Save Those Old Bones

Russ McCarty, senior preparator for the Florida Museum of Natural History in Gainesville, suggests fossil hunters look for shark bite marks on late Miocene and Pliocene marine mammal bones, such as sea cows, whales, and sea lions.

"They are often seen as a series of crescent-shaped scores (bite marks) in the bone," says McCarty. "We have a few pieces of bone that even have the very tips of shark teeth (all *Carcharodon megalodon*) embedded in the bone. It shows what these big sharks were eating.

"It may show a reason for their extinction too. About the time these sharks were munching on baleen whales is about the time that the whales started getting very big themselves ... up to 100-plus feet in the case of blue whales. These whales may just have outgrown Meg and were no longer the little kids on the block."

Many researchers think that whales had become not only larger creatures but better swimmers with improved musculature an tail structure, making them harder to catch. Moreover, they no longer lived in the same place year round but migrated into the Arctic and out of reach of warm-water Megs for greater parts of the year.

Additionally, the Isthmus of Panama rising from the sea altered the Gulf Stream and global circulation, which may have blocked access to Meg's breeding area. Orcas (killer whales), which are highly intelligent mammalian predators (and nearly as big as Meg), evolved to a point where the two of them may have been in direct competition for food.

Sharks and Prehistoric Peoples

Humans throughout prehistory may have always feared sharks, but they also may have always hunted them for food, body ornaments, and tools. In Laura Kozuch's University of Florida master's thesis, "Sharks and Shark Products in Prehistoric South Florida," she asserts that sharks were an important resource for prehistoric peoples.

According to Kozuch, shark teeth were used in wood carvings or shell carvings for utilitarian and ceremonial objects, and were probably traded inland.

Dietary Benefits

Vitamins and nutrients found in shark meat may have been crucial in providing a well-balanced diet to early peoples. Boiled shark fins produce a gelatinous substance that can be used to make soup or glue.

Use of the Skin

As a fine sandpaper, shark skin is great for smoothing out wooden surfaces. The skin is embedded with placoid scales, or dermal denticles, which are firmly embedded in the skin. When Smithsonian archaeologist Frank Hamilton Cushing explored the Gulf Coast of Florida in 1896, he found rolled-up shark skin in the muck at Key Marco, where a wooden figurine that is half human and half cat and other wooden ceremonial objects were also found.

Use of the Teeth

Because there are no stone outcroppings for tools in south Florida, modern shark teeth were useful for cutting and engraving tools. (Fossilized teeth were probably too brittle and dull.) Robin Brown, author of *Florida's First People,* experimented with making tools from modern shark teeth and found them to be better suited than bone or shell. One shark tooth can be used to drill a hole into another. Teeth were then hafted to wooden handles. Cushing also found tiger shark teeth sabers about three feet long at the Key Marco site.

Shark teeth may have been worn as pendants for necklaces. (Vertebrae may have been worn on necklaces or as earrings.)

Sharks ruled in Florida's ancient shallow seas. Photo by Robin Brown.

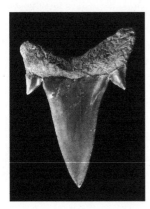

An Eocene extinct mackerel shark tooth (*Otodus obliquus*), Gilchrist County. Photo by Robin Brown.

Extinct giant white (*Carcharodon megalodon*) replica, created by Dr. Cliff Jeremiah. Photo by Robin Brown.

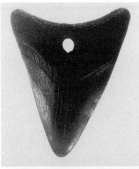

This drilled and polished "Meg" tooth has had at least three lives so far: (1) the shark lost the tooth five to ten million years ago when the state was covered by shallow seas; (2) then it was found by a Native American, perhaps a few thousand years ago, and worn as a pendant, leaving tiny scratch marks and a hole drilled through it; and (3) the author found it in a DeSoto County creek in 1993. Photo by Robin Brown.

Shark vertebra—1 x 1¼ inches, Lee County. Photo by author.

These two extinct giant white (*Carcharodon*) teeth have been polished for sale at the annual Venice Shark Tooth and Seafood Festival. Photo by author.

7

Mammoth Quest

A Search for Giants in Florida

All I can hear is a steady hiss as air bubbles break free from the slow leak in my dive gear's regulator and push their way to the surface. I'm lying on the bottom in four feet of water, gently fanning through the brown tannin-soaked grains of sand to get to the rocks and chunks of bone resting on a layer of limestone a few inches deeper.

Suddenly, I see it, a 12-inch rock that stands out in contrast to the other debris around it. I recognize it immediately as a tooth from an ancient mammoth and just as quickly my heart misses several beats. "Wow," I try to exclaim underwater, but my wife, who is canoeing a few feet away, sees only a few more bubbles.

Upon closer inspection, I also notice the tooth has only eight enamel ridges across the chewing surface, indicating it may be a *Mammuthus hayi*, or Hay's mammoth, a more primitive species that lived near the beginning of the Pleistocene epoch. Had it lived closer to the time that mammoths such as *Mammuthus columbi* became extinct at the end of the Pleistocene, it would have had many more rows of enamel.

Then again, the plate count can only be used on last molars. The tooth I am holding doesn't look like a last molar, so it might be the more progressive species.

I continue to work the spot through a second tank of air and then return two more times the following week. The Peace, like so many Florida rivers, has been exceedingly generous. I uncover another tooth three feet away and several half teeth, none of which match up to each other. I also find large pieces of bone with honeycomb lining, which is typical of mammoth skull. Two-foot bones are in the same area, along with several kneecaps, three vertebrae, rib sections, and pieces of tusk. It was time to break out an O'Doul's and celebrate.

Native Americans called this watery grave of mammoths "Talakchopco hatchee," which means "River of Peas." Somewhere along the way white

A dentist's nightmare. Mammoth (*Mammuthus imperator*) teeth. DeSoto County creek. Photo by author.

Some of the booty. Mammoth teeth collected on the Peace River in Hardee County. Photo by author.

Mammoth (*Mammuthus imperator*) tooth, Peace River. Photo by author.

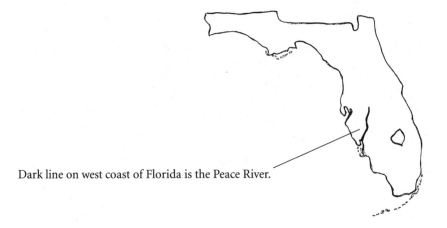

Dark line on west coast of Florida is the Peace River.

settlers changed it to Peace River. Today, 67 miles of the river are a designated canoe trail, beginning at the U.S. Highway 98 bridge just east of Fort Meade and ending downstream at State Road 70 west of Arcadia. There are dozens of places to launch a canoe along the river to begin your own mammoth hunt.

A member of the mammalian order Proboscidea, this huge creature did not resemble a mammoth until about 4 or 5 Ma in Africa. So it's placed in the family Elephantidae.

Orders related to Proboscidea are Hyraxes (a small herbivore) and Sirenia (manatees and dugongs). Within the order Proboscidea, the families for mastodonts and elephants have been separated for most of the Tertiary (at least since the late Eocene some 37.5 Ma).

Florida has been home to various genera of large proboscideans, beginning in the Mid-Miocene epoch 15 Ma, and ending about 10,000 B.P.

The earliest was *Gomphotherium,* which entered North America from Eurasia and settled in Florida about 15 Ma. It had rather straight upper and lower tusks. Another was *Amebelodon,* which also had upper and lower tusks, but they were shaped like shovels, which probably helped it scoop up its vegetarian lunches. A third was *Rhynchotherium,* whose tusks angled down sharply.

Gomphotheriums, or Gomphs, as they're commonly called, began to thin out around the beginning of the Pliocene 5.2 Ma. Only one remained through the end of the Pleistocene 10,000 years B.P.: *Cuvieronius,* which had stubby lower tusks and a spiral enamel band on its upper tusks.

The *Pliomastodons,* which showed up in the Pliocene, led to the Pleistocene genus *Mammut,* which includes the American mastodon (*Mammut americanum*).

At first glance, a mammoth and a mastodon may have looked a lot alike. But a closer look would have shown that the mastodon had a low skull with thick upper tusks and vestigial lower ones. Mammoths, which evolved separately from mastodons, had huge upper tusks, high-domed skulls, and no lower tusks.

There were marked differences between the teeth as well. Mastodons had nipple-shaped crowns suitable for forest browsing, while the mammoths had a flat chewing surface geared more for grassland grazing.

Had it lived long enough, a mammoth might have gone through six sets of four teeth in its lifetime (one tooth for each side of the jaw, upper and lower), with new teeth developing from back to front like a conveyor belt.

Mastodon (*Mammut americanum*) tooth found in Peace River. Photo by author.

When the last set wore out, the animal lost its ability to chew its food thoroughly and soon died.

Mammoths, which belong to the genus *Mammuthus,* arrived in North America about 1.5 Ma and gradually migrated eastward, making their way into Florida. Florida's two Pleistocene species are the Columbian mammoth, or *Mammuthus columbi,* and the imperial mammoth, or *Mammuthus imperator.*

Our state's mammoths were not woolly like their cold-weather counterparts. While some of them reached a height of 13 feet at the shoulders, others, called dwarf mammoths, evolved independently on at least three islands around the globe. They were between three and six feet tall.

When the first humans arrived in Florida a little over 12,000 years ago, mammoths were among the dominant species inhabiting Earth. Theories abound as to how and why they became extinct, especially since two species were involved and the extinctions occurred at different times, in different areas.

Certainly, humans sought them out (dead or alive) to make tools and weapons from their bones and tusks, and for food. It's possible mammoths were hunted into extinction, but many researchers believe they probably became extinct because of a combination of climatic and human factors. Major changes in climate and vegetation may have forced the animals into small populations in areas of remaining habitat (drought, for example, would have driven them to the last water holes), making them easy prey for such hunters as humans and large carnivores.

The mammoth range began to shrink about 25,000 years ago, with the larger animals dying out in Europe, North America, and Siberia around 10,000 to 12,000 years ago, and the dwarf mammoths disappearing off Siberia's Wrangel Island about 4,000 years ago.

Mammoths may be gone, but as long as Florida has such a rich record of their existence here, they will forever be resurrected.

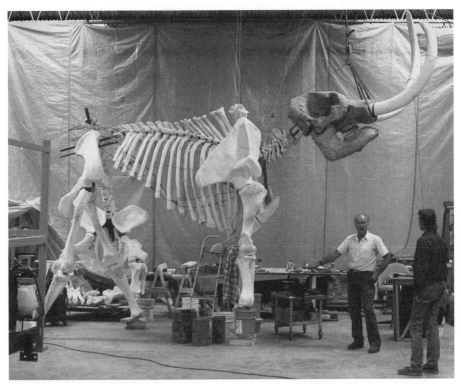

"Priscilla," a cast of an American mastodon (*Mammut americanum*), made by Don Serbosek (who also found the animal while diving in the Aucilla River) and Dr. Cliff Jeremiah. Photo by author.

Mammoth teeth fragments and a rusty pistol. (Do you suppose the gun was used to . . . ? Never mind.) Orange River, Lee County. Photo by author.

Mammoth (*Mammuthus imperator*) tooth, Peace River. Photo by author.

Juvenile mammoth (*Mammuthus columbi*) tooth, Peace River. Photo by author.

Cast of juvenile mammoth (species unknown) tooth. Photo by author.

Cast of gomphothere (*Cuvieronius tropicus*) tooth. Gomphotheres were elephantlike animals with upper and lower tusks. Photo by author.

Mastodon (*Mammut americanum*) tooth found in DeSoto County creek. Photo by author.

American mastodon (*Mammut americanum*) tooth, Peace River, Hardee County. Photo by author.

The Peace River during the tranquil winter dry season. Photo by author.

Juvenile mastodon (*Mammut americanum*) tooth, Orange River. Photo by author.

Dugong Dynasty

Tripping over a 10-Million-Year-Old Sea Cow

Had you been alive to visit the southern tip of Florida 10 Ma, you wouldn't have found yourself strolling along the white, sandy beaches of Miami or plowing through the Everglades saw grass in a fast-moving airboat. Those areas were under the ocean, due to a global rise in sea levels brought on by melting polar ice caps. In fact, the Miocene's Miami was actually 250 miles north of that city, near the present-day town of Fort Meade in Polk County.

Thick forests and grassy plains covered the stubby peninsula of Florida during the Mid-Miocene. In this subtropical environment you would have encountered shovel-tusked mastodons, hornless rhinoceroses, and humpless camels. Tortoises six feet across, iguanas, gila monsters, and 30-foot crocodiles all thrived in this epoch as well. Offshore, the warm shallow seas were teeming with long-beaked dolphins, bony fish, sharks, rays, and sea cows.

Dugong site after all the bones were removed and Cargill began its reclamation process. Photo by author.

A few years ago, I was able to journey back into the Mid-Miocene and visit southern Florida's ancient tip by way of an abandoned Polk County phosphate mine. What I found took me completely by surprise. A horizontal line of pale white, heart-shaped vertebrae and broken ribs lay exposed in the walls of one of the mines. Miraculously, the bones had only been grazed by the huge claw of a dragline bucket just before the mine closed down. I suspected the bones belonged to a dugong, or *Metaxytherium floridanum*, but wasn't sure at the time. The dugong is a saltwater cousin to today's West Indian manatee.

The operators of the mine, Cargill Fertilizer, gave the local fossil club I headed permission to excavate. We were ecstatic. But the Florida Museum of Natural History had no staff paleontologist available to spend any quality time overseeing the project. Besides, the museum staff informed us, the odds were pretty slim that any more of the skeleton would be found in the wall, let alone the entire animal.

They recommended we enlist the aid of Barbara Toomey, who, together with her son, Jim, volunteered to spearhead the project. Barbara is known not only for volunteering her time and money for worthwhile paleo-archaeological causes, but for using professional excavating techniques.

Cargill's time machine, a giant motorized shovel, finished scraping away several million years of accumulated life and death in just a few hours. Now we were only a few inches above the level in which one of the world's most gentle creatures lay buried.

Over the ensuing weeks, the Toomeys, Sue Watts, and a few other volunteers used pickaxes and garden trowels to get even closer to the bones. Then it was time to break out the dental picks.

We held our breath as each vertebra led to another and then another. With dugongs, the skull, flippers, and tail section were the most important parts, but often the first to get washed away. Would they be there when we dug back that far? How long would our luck hold out?

The vertebrae we had exposed were covered with a blue-green phosphatic clay that had kept the bones intact since the animal died. To scrape off all the clay could cause the bones to crumble when it was time to re-

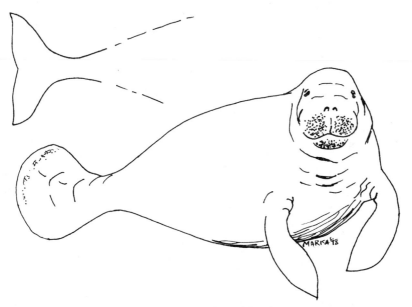

Comparison of dugong (top) and manatee (bottom) tails.

move them. From the partial vertebrae showing through, we assumed we would soon uncover the tail section—if it was there.

Before long, we heard a metallic sound from a volunteer's trowel; it was the blade scraping against fossilized bone. A dental pick was used to clear off more clay, and to our surprise a row of six worn rectangular teeth was exposed. Instead of the tail, we had uncovered the skull!

Gary Morgan, a former senior biologist of vertebrate paleontology at the Florida Museum, was able to positively identify the animal from photographs of the teeth. There was no doubt it was a dugong, an extinct representative of the sirenians, or sea cows. Morgan said the bones were approximately 10 million years old. Dugongs became extinct here 2 to 3 Ma, about the same time that manatees moved into Florida. Dugongs are still present in Asian waters. The fossil record of sirenians begins 50 Ma.

This animal had come to rest upside down. The lower jaw had slid off to the side, exposing the teeth in the upper jaw. As the days wore on, more of the dugong was uncovered, including most of the tail vertebrae. By the time work was halted, 85 percent of the 12-foot-long skeleton had been located and removed.

Unlike today's West Indian manatee, some dugongs sported tusks up to a foot long in their upper jaws. Resembling daggers or hoes, the tusks were used to uproot sea grasses and possibly to battle other dugongs. The one we were uncovering had no tusks. Rather than the round, paddlelike tail flipper found on manatees, the dugong's was broad like that of a whale.

It appeared as if the animal had not died alone. Within 500 feet of the site, the partial skeletons of more dugongs were found.

"It may have been a Miocene cold snap that killed them," says Morgan. "We really don't know for sure. They may have died in a coastal lagoon or estuary, perhaps between barrier islands and the coast."

Other theories are that the dugongs may have died collectively of a disease, or perhaps the bones accumulated over a period of a hundred years or more, even though they were found at about the same level.

"The water was probably about 20 feet deep at the time," Morgan continues. "We're standing 125 feet above sea level right now, so that means the ocean would have been 145 feet higher than it is today." He estimates that Florida is 180 miles longer today than it was when the dugong lived.

Typical dragline bucket, Mulberry Museum. Photo by Marisa Renz.

A West Indies Manatee, cousin to the dugong, in a canal at Port of the Isles in the Everglades. Photo by author.

Noting the blue-green clay surrounding the bones, Morgan says that "clay means quiet waters. The material is more compact and finer than sand, which indicates there wasn't much tidal action here. Currents weren't real strong."

Mixed in with the dugong bones was evidence that other sea life existed at the same time. Sand dollars, eagle ray teeth, whale and sawfish vertebrae, snouts from long-beaked dolphins and lemon shark teeth were recovered, along with a bony armor plate from an extinct crocodile known as a *Gavialosuchus.*

In the same area, at a slightly higher elevation and in black soil, we found bones and teeth from prehistoric horses, camels, mammoths, and bison—indicating a more recent time when the ocean had receded and Florida's seas reached their present-day level.

While unearthing the dugong, we wrapped each rib (some in as many as 20 pieces) in aluminum foil and labeled it so the skeleton would be easier to reconstruct later. Groups of vertebrae and the skull were plaster-jacketed to ensure they wouldn't come apart once removed from the site.

Today, the repaired parts of the skeleton are filed in a drawer in the bowels of the Florida Museum of Natural History. My first thoughts, upon hearing this, were "Whoa, what do you mean they're buried in some back room? Why aren't they on display in the museum?" But once I got my ego in check, I realized that the bones were in the best possible place, where they could be of greatest use to science. My reasoning was as follows:

First, the university already had a partial skeleton on display in its museum. Second, once bone hardener has been applied to a skeleton, holes drilled, and mounting racks attached, it makes it difficult to study the original material, because it's been altered. Third, once a skeleton is on display, scientific study becomes more difficult for there is not adequate work space on a museum floor and the public watches the researcher's every move. Fourth, and finally, keeping the skeleton in my own possession was simply not an option. Can you imagine the logistics, time, and expense involved if professionals had to visit every amateur's living room around the state (not to mention the amateurs who leave the state with their finds) to examine each fossil of interest?

Dugong skull cast from the collection of the Florida Museum of Natural History, Gainesville. Photo by author.

The dugong is a significant find, according to Morgan, because articulated—or joined—fossilized skeletons of any animal are rare, especially those with intact skulls and jaws. In the case of this species of dugong, scientists at the time had never found as much of a skeleton as we had, so our specimen offered them the opportunity to closely study certain bones they had never seen before.

While articulated skeletons are rare finds, isolated bones from dugongs are so common that in certain Florida creeks and rivers their fossilized ribs are stacked together as if they had been dumped there by the semitrailer load.

Imagine looking out over a bay 10 Ma and seeing hundreds of dugongs as they surface for air before diving again to feed on underwater vegetation. Imagine, too, a sea garden lush enough to support so many of these massive, slow-moving creatures at one time. I would love to have witnessed it. I feel as if I have.

The phosphate deposits below the dugong graveyard are 10 to 15 million years old. Phosphate itself is an organic compound. The substance is used

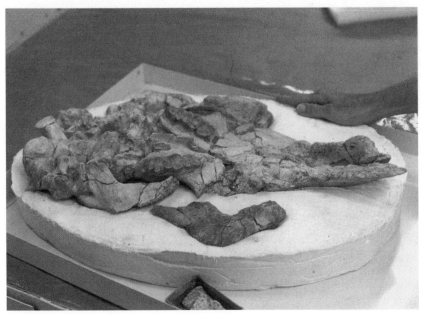

The dugong skull was badly crushed. Note row of teeth at center of photo. Photo by author.

in fertilizer, soda, camera film, plastics, shaving cream, bone china dishes, and lightbulbs. It makes steel harder and water softer, and plays a role in dyeing cloth and washing clothes. Phosphate is in the cement dentists use on teeth and the fluids used to drill for oil and gas.

The large area in which the dugong was found is called Bone Valley because so many fossils have turned up there. It covers parts of Polk, Hardee, Manatee, Hillsborough, and Highlands counties.

Once Cargill finishes its excavations for phosphate, the company usually fills in the pits with sand and topsoil, then plants grass or citrus trees. When I recently viewed the dugong site, it looked as if the company's time machines had never even disturbed the land.

Some of the ribs after restoration by preparator Russ McCarty at the Florida Museum of Natural History. Photo by author.

Cargill grade-all clearing overburden at dugong site. Photo by author.

The blue-green clay meant "quiet waters," says Gary Morgan, former senior biologist of vertebrate paleontology at the Florida Museum of Natural History. Photo by author.

There were other dugong skeletons, as well as whale bones nearby. Photo by Ray Seguin.

Thunder Lizard

Coexisting with a Remarkable Living Fossil

I had a feeling I was being watched. For the last hour, my face had been buried in three feet of water as I snorkeled the shallows in search of fossils. Preoccupied with scanning the creek bed, I hadn't noticed him until it was too late. Suddenly, I was within 10 feet of a 12-foot, 500-pound bull alligator, his dark menacing eyes locked into mine. Not only was I too close, but he was on dry land while I was wading in his domain.

Resisting the temptation to scream and get the hell out of the water as fast as I could, I told myself to relax, to keep my eyes on him, and to back up slowly. Easier thought than done. In the middle of my first step backward, my foot snagged on a branch underwater and I was thrown off balance, creating a large splash as I sank completely under the surface.

Hurriedly, I stood up again, my head breaking the surface just in time to see the massive flesh-eating reptile shoot off the bank like a missile, covering me with a wall of water.

Alligators sunning themselves on a pond bank in the Everglades. Photo by author.

This is it, I remember thinking as I tried to regain my balance. But as the water calmed, I saw no sign of him. I continued backing up until the water was only a few inches deep, then climbed the bank to safety.

I had just learned a very valuable lesson (be more careful!) and had witnessed alligator behavior that is more the norm than an exception. This bony-plated animal, more than twice my length and weight, with 80 conical teeth protruding an inch out of its powerful jaws, was actually afraid of me.

Unless an alligator has been fed by humans, its natural tendency is to avoid us. Consider the following statistics: From 1973 to 1997, there have been fewer than 200 documented alligator attacks on people in Florida. Nine of them were fatal. Over the same period, hundreds of thousands of people splashed around in our rivers and lakes without being harmed by these creatures. While we certainly should respect an alligator for what it can do, our fears and imaginations are much larger than real life.

Family Tree

As the largest living reptile, the alligator has a family tree that goes back millions of years and that is similar to the dinosaur's. Both were part of a group of small reptiles known as Thecodontia, which dominated Earth's primordial swamps and seas 250 Ma during the Mesozoic era. Averaging less than five feet in length, thecodonts had back legs much longer than the front ones, suggesting they were bipedal (like many dinosaurs that walked upright). Another trait they shared with dinosaurs was the two large temporal openings in their skulls.

Alligators are grouped under the order Crocodilia, which includes 23 species. Crododilians are divided into three families: true crocodiles; caimans and alligators; and gharials. About 60 Ma, true crocodiles and alligators diverged from each other.

Here in Florida, the reptile we know as *Alligator mississippiensis* has inhabited our state for only 10 million years, since the Miocene epoch. It is one of only two living species of alligators in the world. The other is the rare Chinese alligator (*Alligator sinensis*) of the Yangtze River.

The caimans of Central and South America are the only other members of the alligator group, differing from alligators in the structure of their scutes. An introduced population of spectacled caimans (*Caiman crocodilus*) occupies some man-made canals in south Florida, near Homestead.

What do crocodilians, birds, and dinosaurs have in common? All three have been placed in a subclass called Archosauria, because their behavior is similar. They each build nests, care for their young, and communicate vocally. The young also follow their mother around like ducklings, often resting on her back.

Did You Know . . . ?

- Alligators can live as long as 50 years in the wild, longer in captivity. An alligator in captivity in St. Augustine is thought to be 100 years old.

Alligator scutes (osteoderms), which function like miniature solar panels to draw in the sun's rays. Orange River, Lee County. Photo by author.

- Fish make up most of an alligator's diet. Alligators also enjoy turtles, snakes, crabs, birds, and other small animals, including dogs and cats.
- Alligators eat an average of one meal per week in the spring and summer, sometimes not at all during the winter months.
- They will not eat when temperatures drop below about 60 degrees Fahrenheit because there is not enough heat to activate their digestive enzymes. Cold weather can kill an alligator with a full stomach, for the food will rot instead of digest.
- If necessary, adults can live for six months or longer without food by utilizing the fat stored in their tails.
- An alligator acts like a submarine before submerging. A third eyelid allows it to see underwater, its ear slits and nostrils seal shut, and if it grabs prey under the surface, a flap in the back of the throat prevents water from entering its lungs.
- Alligators can remain underwater for over an hour. Like humans, they have a four-chambered heart, but when submerged they re-

route their blood to reduce circulation to the lungs, which helps them stay under longer.

• An alligator can lay as few as 20 eggs and as many as 60. Wading birds, owls, hawks, raccoons, otters, and bobcats will eat 80 percent of the young. Once an alligator reaches maturity, the roles of predator and prey are reversed.

• The temperature inside the egg determines the sex. If it's above 89 degrees Fahrenheit, it will probably be a male; a lower temperature will produce a female.

• Rather than sitting on their nests like chickens, alligators cover the eggs with wet plants that incubate the eggs as they decompose.

• Mother alligators are among the best moms in nature because they protect their young upwards of three years. Food is a different matter, as the babies must find their own insects and minnows until they're large enough for bigger prey.

• The osteoderms, or bony scutes on their backs, not only serve to protect them but also act as miniature solar panels to take in the sun's rays. In this way, alligators store energy from the sun.

• An alligator does not have a brain, but rather a cerebral cortex, or brain stem. Contrary to popular belief that they are dumb reptiles, alligators are instilled with a predator intelligence that has enabled them to outlive dinosaurs. They are smart and highly adaptive to changing environments.

• Water temperature determines their habitat selection; usually shallow water where they can best maintain an optimum body temperature of about 89 degrees Fahrenheit.

• Teeth are replaced quickly when lost, just as with sharks, and they can produce up to 6,000 in a 50-year life. Their jaws can slam shut with as much pressure as 2,000 pounds per square inch. They have no molars. Instead, their conical-shaped teeth enable them to tear.

• Early American colonists sometimes used the teeth to hold gunpowder, and in the 1800s, teeth were polished and mounted in silver and sold in jewelry stores as baby pacifiers.

• Whether an animal flies or swims, it is going to have trouble spotting an alligator. Not only do alligators look like half-submerged

A handful of fossilized alligator teeth found in a DeSoto County creek. Photo by author.

logs floating in the water, but from the air they are often as dark as the black water they inhabit. If you were a fish looking up at an alligator's belly, you might miss it because it's light colored like the sky.

• One of the largest alligators on record was killed at Apopka, Florida, in 1956. It measured 17 feet, 5 inches. Louisiana holds the record for the biggest, in 1890: 19 feet, 2 inches.

Was That an Alligator or a Crocodile?

Crocodiles prefer salt water, whereas alligators can usually be found in freshwater ponds, marshes, and swamps. Both have been found in brackish water, which is a mixture of the two. To tell them apart, look first at the snout. The crocodile's is long and narrow, almost pointed. The alligator's is shaped more like a shovel blade. Count the teeth if you dare. Alligators have 80, crocodiles around 70. Also look for the fourth tooth back on the lower jaw of the crocodile. It will be very pronounced.

Hunting Alligators

There is a hunting season for alligators in the fall. Through a lottery system about 500 people get the opportunity to match wits with these ancient predators. It's not much of a challenge, though, because it is easy to get within a few feet of them at night using spotlights. To make it more of a match, perhaps hunters should seek them out without the benefit of clothing, weapons, boats, or mosquito repellent. Hunters would have to swim in the swamp at night with no lights, and with a stringer full of dead fish tied to their waists to attract them. No alligators under 12 feet could be taken.

Seriously, controlled hunts are believed to be the most effective way to protect alligators and their habitats. Profits from hunting licenses (which run $250 for residents and $1,000 for out-of-staters) and tag fees help support alligator-management programs and population surveys. The hunters are allowed to sell the hides for profit.

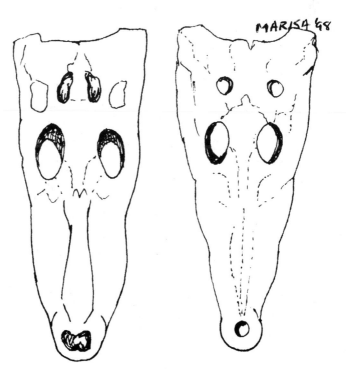

Comparison of alligator and crocodile (narrower) skulls.

Think Safety When Fossiling

Almost all Florida creeks, rivers, and canals are a potential habitat for alligators. So when you collect fossils in the water, you would do well to follow a few helpful hints:

- Don't collect in the early morning or just before dusk; that's when alligators are most likely to be active. Scope out the banks before getting in the water. Are there tail drag marks in the sand?
- Are the grasses or reeds flattened out on the shoreline, suggesting something large has been resting there? Is there a lot of vegetation such as water hyacinths growing in the water close to shore? That's a perfect place for a large alligator to hide.
- Never feed an alligator because then it can't tell the hand from the handout and it loses its fear of humans. This is the most dangerous type of alligator.

Management and Conservation

Alligators now number over 20,000 in the Everglades, over one million for the state, and another million and a half for the rest of the Southeast. Crocodiles, in comparison, number fewer than 500, most of which are in the Florida Keys.

Populations today are managed through farms and ranches, controlled hunts, a nuisance-alligator program (which should be called a nuisance-people program because so many people feed them, making them more dangerous), and habitat protection.

Alligators are seen as a renewable resource with considerable commercial value. The goal is to harvest no more than can be replaced by the population's normal reproduction. Over 150 large-scale alligator programs are being run in several states. The meat sells for five to seven dollars per pound to restaurants and wholesalers, and the skins go for $25 or more per linear foot to leather tanneries throughout the world.

Myths and Reality

Over the centuries, some native American tribes have worshiped alligators. Teeth and bones were worked into awls and vials, and teeth worn like a necklace to prevent illnesses. Alligator hides were sometimes used for ceremonial drums, and entrails were woven into baskets. There is a 700-foot-long alligator effigy mound at Grand Lake, Louisiana.

Legends about fire-breathing dragons may have originated with alligators. Among the superstitions connected with alligators are the following: Rubbing alligator fat on limbs aching from rheumatism will bring relief. Colonists in North Carolina believed that male impotence could be cured by eating the teeth of an alligator's right jaw. They also thought that eating ashes from burned alligator skin soaked in oil had narcotic effects.

Where Are They?

Alligators—The alligator we know today as *Alligator mississippiensis* has inhabited Florida since the Miocene epoch about 10 Ma. Alligators inhabited Europe until about 3 Ma, when cold weather drove them out. Five hundred thousand years ago, they lived as far north as Maryland, and today the bulk of them inhabit Florida, southern Georgia, Louisiana, and parts of Texas. On a smaller scale, they can be found in Alabama, Arkansas, Mississippi, North and South Carolina, and even Oklahoma.

Crocodiles—The endangered American Crocodile (*Crocodylus acutus*) can be found in Central America, northern South America, the Caribbean, Jamaica, Cuba, and the southern tip of Florida (Fort Lauderdale to Sanibel Island, including Florida Bay and northern Key Largo).

Who Needs Alligators?

You name the plant or animal, and it's bound to have a role—however indirectly—in benefiting humans. It's no different with the alligator.

Don't like mosquitoes? Believe it or not, alligators actually help control their numbers. As the dry season gets under way, alligators dig holes into the water table. Not only do these holes become an oasis for countless animals that might otherwise have to walk miles for a drink, but they provide a habitat for a small mosquito-eating fish called a gambusia, which can eat up to 300 mosquito larvae an hour. So more alligators mean more gambusia and fewer mosquitoes.

By digging out areas before the water in them completely dries out, alligators ensure that the fish, minnows, and other critters stay alive throughout the dry season. When the first rains hit, the water spills out into the swamp, dispersing all this cooped-up life, and keeps the cycle going.

In addition to assisting humans, alligators help protect bird rookeries by eating raccoons that attempt to swim to river islands to climb trees and steal bird eggs. Alligators also spread valuable nutrients throughout the swamp with their bowel movements, which become food for certain plants and small organisms.

From Many to Few to Many to . . . What's Next?

Alligators, which were here before many dinosaurs, very nearly became extinct by 1967, thanks to another species: humans. Greed, vanity, and consumerism were the reasons, beginning as far back as 1855. Ten million hides were processed between 1870 and 1965. Alligators were used for food as well, and their oil was even used to lubricate machinery in the cotton industry.

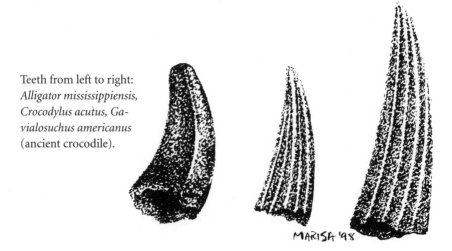

Teeth from left to right: *Alligator mississippiensis, Crocodylus acutus, Gavialosuchus americanus* (ancient crocodile).

Scutes from left to right: *Alligator mississippiensis, Crocodylus acutus, Gavialosuchus americanus.*

As noted earlier, due to management and conservation efforts, their total numbers are over two and a half million. Even though they were taken off the endangered species list in 1987, they're still protected.

Crocodiles, on the other hand, remain on the endangered species list, with fewer than 500 left. Their habitats are saltwater and brackish water coastlines, which have been drastically reduced because that's where the majority of people who move to Florida—some 1,000 per day—settle.

Alligator's hide. Notice the scutes (osteoderms), or ridges, lining the back. Photo by author.

When fossiling, look for obvious signs that there may be a gator nearby, such as tail drag marks on a sandy bank, or flat areas on the banks a gator may have used for sunning. Photo by author.

These reptiles are not out of the swamp yet. It remains to be seen whether pollution and loss of habitat will again bring on a major decline in their numbers—only this time it may not be so easy to turn things around. In Lake Apopka, the third largest lake in Florida, a chemical spill and ongoing agricultural pesticide contamination have been linked to reproductive problems with alligators and largemouth bass.

And Lake Apopka is but a microcosm of other Florida lakes and wetlands. If current trends continue, alligators run the risk of being wiped out by pollution. And if alligators and fish are affected, it's just a matter of time before humans are, too.

The alligator has a rounded jaw shaped like a shovel blade, while the croc's is narrower.

Want to attract an alligator? Bring your dog with you to a river or creek. Dogs are usually low to the ground and often resemble other animals that are the alligator's natural prey: raccoons and river otters. Dogs also tend to be noisy and splash around, which excites alligators. Photo of author's dog, Coonie, by Marisa Renz.

10 ◎

Here Today, Gone Yesterday

Florida's Fossil Horse Trail

What do the history of horses and the changing of the weather have in common? A lot. If you look back over the last 55 million years, you'll find that climatic changes have played a major role in the evolution of many animals, not just the horse.

Much of North America from 58 to 30 Ma was forests and woodlands. A small, two-foot-tall mammal called *Hyracotherium* (also known as *Eohippus,* ancestor to all horses) ducked in and out of these areas as it browsed on berries, buds, and leaves. Because of its diet, *Hyracotherium* had low-crowned teeth. It had four toes on the front limbs and three in back. Two to four species of horses coexisted during this time.

Then, from 30 Ma to about 11,000 years B.P., evolution sent the horses in countless directions, with many trails overlapping. It's not unusual in some fossil sites today to uncover as many as 10 different species of horse.

Author getting a wet one from Blanche, a gentle descendant of the horses (*Equus*) the Spanish conquistadors reintroduced to the Americas in the 1500s. Photo by Marisa Renz.

Horses Grow Up

About 20 Ma, gradual shifts in Earth's weather patterns forced some of the woodlands and forests to transform into grassy savannas. As the vegetation changed, so did horses by developing high-crowned teeth better suited for grasslands grazing. (Although recent studies show some horses ate only grass, some ate a mix of grass, leaves, and shrubs, and the modern-like *Dinohippus* ate mostly from trees and shrubs.) Horses also began to lose their side toes, resulting in single hooves, and some species grew much larger than their predecessors.

Why the longer legs and fewer toes? A miniature horse would be ideally suited for finding food and hiding from predators in a woodsy environment, but out in the open, longer legs and greater speed would be more effective to escape prey.

As long-term global environments continued to shift from hot to cold and back again, horses became less diverse. By 2 Ma, *Equus* and *Nannippus* were the only remaining horses in North America. Some *Equus* migrated to the Old World across the Bering Strait Land Bridge about 3 Ma, but they had become extinct in North and South America by 10,000 years B.P.

As mentioned in an earlier chapter, it's possible horses and other large animals were hunted into extinction, but many researchers believe it's more likely that they became extinct because of a combination of climatic and human factors.

It's interesting to note that North America is the starting point for horses, and that they spread to other parts of the world before being wiped out here. And now they're back again, thanks to a reintroduction by the Spanish conquistadors in the early 1500s.

First Horses in Florida

Because most of Florida was under water in the early days of the horse, our first record of this animal here is about 25 to 30 Ma. Sounding more like a scientific name for hippos, *Mesohippus* was a three-toed plant eater about the size of a collie. It was first discovered at the I-75 site in the mid-1960s, as I-75 was being constructed just south of Gainesville.

During the Miocene epoch 23.3 to 5.2 Ma, Florida horses became more varied. There were enough of the tiny three-toed *Parahippus* fossils present in Gilchrist County that a complete skeleton was assembled. Larger and more primitive was the browser *Anchitherium*, which crossed the Bering land bridge and colonized Eurasia.

For the last half of the Miocene, Florida three-toed horses were called *Hipparions*, which included *Hipparion, Cormohipparion, Neohipparion,*

Astragalus (ankle) bone.
Photo by author.

Equus tooth. Photo by author.

and *Nannippus.* Their teeth look much like those of *Equus,* the Pleistocene horse of 1.68 Ma to 10,000 years B.P., except they are smaller and have an isolated island of enamel called a protocone in their upper molars.

Five to 12 Ma, a tiny three-toed horse called *Pseudhipparion* spent most of its evolutionary life in Florida, surviving two or three million years longer here than on the Great Plains. By the end of the Miocene about 5 Ma, *Astrohippus* and *Dinohippus* (probably a direct ancestor to *Equus*) began to look a lot like our modern horses. Neither had useful side toes.

At the beginning of the Pliocene 5 Ma, most of the three-toed horses vanished. *Nannippus* lived until the end of the Pliocene as *Equus* was first appearing. Had *Equus* not found its way across the Bering land bridge to Europe, the Spaniards would have been horseless when they first set foot on our beaches.

Big Birds and Little Horses

Tiny three-toed horses during the Pliocene may have had an unlikely predator. Named after noted collector Ben Waller, *Titanus walleri* was an imposing carnivorous bird that stood between 6 and 10 feet tall. Its bill may have been lined with razor-sharp teeth, and it may have dined on three-toed horses, literally running them down in short bursts of speed up to 50 miles per hour.

Comparing toe bones. Left to right: mammoth/sloth toe bone (top row), bison/deer/camel toe bone (middle row), horse/tortoise toe bone (bottom row).

How Do You Know You've Found a Horse Tooth?

Because it's a grassland grazer, a horse's teeth today are high crowned. But 58 Ma, *Hyracotherium*'s teeth were low crowned because it was a woodland browser. On each side of its jaw were three incisors, one canine, four premolars, and three molars. About 20–25 Ma, it lost or reduced the size of its first premolar, so now the formula is 3–1–3–3, or a total of 40 teeth in the modern horse.

Each tooth is given an abbreviation: *I* for incisor, *C* for canine, *P* for premolar, *M* for molar on the upper jaw; and *i, c, p, m* for the correspond-

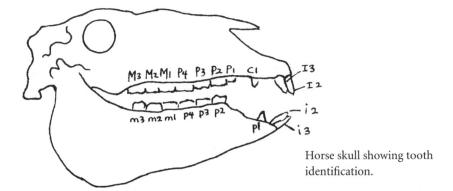

Horse skull showing tooth identification.

ing teeth on the lower jaw. So an LP2 is on the left side of the upper jaw; it's an upper premolar and is the second one back.

Something to Chew On

Like many mammals, the horse produces two sets of incisors, canines, and premolars. The first set are referred to as "deciduous," while the second set are "permanent." Molars develop in single sets, usually erupting as the deciduous premolars are being dropped.

A Few Fossil Horse Sites

Thomas Farm in Gilchrist County held one of the richest bone beds in North America. A member of the Florida Geological Survey stumbled upon the site, which is believed to be an ancient sinkhole. Over 30 species of mammals have been found, including horses such as *Parahippus leonensis* and *Archaeohippus*.

Leisey shell pit, near Ruskin in Hillsborough County, produced three species of genus *Equus*. Discovered by noted collector Frank Garcia, these were among the first horses to develop a locking mechanism, whereby the tendon of the biceps muscle locks in the upper arm bone (humerus), thus allowing horses to stand for long periods of time without their muscles getting tired. Also from this site, Terry and Margaret Sellari uncovered a "paleo pathological" femur of *Equus*. The femur indicated that when the animal lived, it had suffered from an acute case of arthritis.

A Pinellas County site contained an articulated (fully joined) skeleton of a 25-million-year-old *Miohippus* (Miocene three-toed horse). Discovered by avid collector Chris Skillman, it was excavated by Tampa Bay Fossil Club volunteers Tony Estevez, Bob Vander Gronden, Steve Jacobson, Terry Sellari, Frank Kocsis, and Sharon Blinebury.

Surprise Cave in Alachua County is a 10,000-year-old time capsule with an *Equus* astragalus (ankle bone), calcaneum (heel bone), and tooth. The site was discovered by Florida Museum of Natural History paleontologist Art Poyer.

DeSoto site in Hardee County has produced specimens of the tiny dwarf horse *Nannippus*, and Steve and Roxanne Wilson contributed to the Florida

Museum of Natural History a unique upper molar of *Pseudhipparion*, another dwarf horse. Collector Suzan Hutchens found fossils of *Nannippus* at the same site.

Moss Acres Racetrack in Marion County turned up seven-million-year-old remains of *Cormohipparion* and *Calippus maccartyi*, and *Nannippus*, found by paleontologists from the Florida Museum.

Gardinier Mine in the Bone Valley area includes mandibles and maxillae of early Pliocene (*Hemphillian*) horses and rare middle Miocene horse teeth, as well as an astragalus from a primitive browsing horse (*Hypohippus* or *Megahippus*).

Horse Exhibit

Thanks to bones collected from the Thomas Farm site and funds made available from the state of Florida, a dwarf-horse *Archaeohippus* skeleton has been added to the University of Florida's new fossil horse exhibit. Steve and Suzan Hutchens (who reconstructed the Leisey *Equus* for the same exhibit) completed the job of articulating the skeleton.

The horse exhibit is part of the Hall of Florida Fossils in the Florida Museum of Natural History Exhibits and Education Center in Powell Hall on 34th Street in Gainesville.

Modern (*Equus*) horse jaw with a fossilized (*Equus*) tooth.

A handful of horse (*Equus*) teeth, Peace River, Hardee County. Photo by author.

Equus mandible belonging to veteran collector Frank Garcia. Photo by Robin Brown.

Equus mandible with two teeth, found in DeSoto County creek. Photo by author.

Horse cannon bone (metatarsal) and toe bones.

11

Florida's Fossil Felines

Saber-toothed Cats, Jaguars, and Lions

Although he outweighed his attacker by six tons, the unsuspecting mammoth was no match for the crafty saber-toothed cat. The vicious carnivore, a third again the size of an African lion, lunged up at her prey and sank her eight-inch-long sabers through the mammoth's inch-thick hide.

Pulling back with massive neck muscles, the huge cat ripped open the vulnerable underbelly, exposing the internal organs. As suddenly as she had attacked, she leaped away from the mammoth, avoiding his menacing 10-foot tusks and enormous feet that could easily have trampled her smaller body. Patiently, she and the rest of the pride followed the wounded animal until it keeled over from a loss of blood. Then, methodically, they moved in for the kill.

Even though paleontologists can only theorize about this type of prey-predator relationship between these two prehistoric creatures, one thing is for certain. Both animals existed throughout the world, including Florida.

Which Big Cats Were in Florida?

The first catlike animals to stalk prey in Florida appeared nine Ma in the middle Miocene epoch. *Barbourofelis,* or false saber-toothed cat as it's called, reached about 120 pounds, with curved, flat upper canine teeth.

At the same time, another larger cat, *Nimravides,* patrolled the wilds of Florida's woods and grasslands. It was built more like a jaguar and instead of flat-bladed sabers, was equipped with sharp, but rounded canines.

Two of its cousins, *Megantereon* and *Machairodus,* evolved in Eurasia. *Megantereon* arrived in Florida about 5 to 6 Ma and was the smallest of Florida's Plio-Pleistocene sabercats. It appears to have evolved into the medium-sized sabercat, *Smilodon gracilis,* in the late Pliocene between 2 and 3 Ma. *Smilodon gracilis* lived in Florida from the late Pliocene to the middle of the Pleistocene (about 3 Ma to 300,000 years ago).

The large sabercat *Smilodon floridanus* (also known as *Smilodon populator* and *Smilodon fatalis*) appeared in Florida in the late Pleistocene about 300,000 years ago. A Pleistocene lion, half again the size of today's African lions, also competed for large prey. *Panthera atrox* (also known as *Felis atrox*) is actually related to today's house cats.

Evolution and Saber-toothed Cats

Evolution, while appearing to be a confusing and mixed-up process, is actually very precise if you look at the big picture. As environments and food sources change, animals like the saber-toothed cat are forced to adapt to the change, move to another area, or gradually become extinct.

Those that adapt may grow longer or shorter legs, larger or smaller teeth, which may be flatter or rounder than in previous generations. They may increase or decrease in body weight, develop more acute hearing in dense woods or better eyesight on open plains. They may have longer gestation periods, shorter nursing times, or more or less participation from their extended family in nurturing the young into adulthood and in hunting routines.

The animals that relocate because of environmental changes, including a disruption in the quantity or quality of food available, will seek out habitats similar to their old way of life. If they don't find them, or they are unable to adjust to the changes, inevitably their species may die out.

Evolution is an effective but sometimes harsh process. It places demands on all living creatures to change with the world around them, to develop stronger, more versatile genes as needs dictate. It is constantly striving for perfection, influencing the smallest atom to the whole of the cosmos. Even with all its harshness, it's still a beautiful process.

What Is a False Saber-toothed Cat?

Although cats didn't show up in Florida until 9 Ma, they have been part of the fossil record elsewhere for 30 million years, since the Oligocene epoch.

Some of the early cats, such as *Nimravidae*, are no longer considered true cats because of slight skeletal differences. True cats, like today's lion and house cats, have an auditory bulla, which allows sound to travel to the brain.

In true cats, the interior of the bulla is separated into two chambers, whereas nimravids lacked separations or the entire bulla. Instead, many scientists believe, nimravids had a cartilaginous housing for the ear mechanism that did not fossilize. False cats would have evolved at the same time as true cats but would not be a direct ancestor.

MARISA '97

What Makes a Carnivore a Carnivore?

By definition, a carnivore is an animal that consumes mostly meat, or other creatures with backbones. And it should also have at least one pair of specialized carnassial teeth for slicing the meat. But not all carnivores are carnivorous. Pandas, for instance, eat bamboo, badgers will eat both meat and greens—meaning they are omnivorous—and the aardwolf is an ant and termite eater. Humans, on the other hand, are primates, yet we certainly consume our share of meat. Wild pigs will occasionally eat small animals but are not considered carnivores.

True and false cats fit the definition well with their agility, speed, intelligence, and sharp teeth. In saber-toothed cats, the sabers caused other modifications in the skull and jaws. They had short faces and strong neck muscles, with a lower jaw that dropped nearly straight down for the sabers to clear the biting surface and strike. Some sabers had serrated edges to tear as they sliced.

How Did Saber-toothed Cats Kill?

Some researchers claim saber-toothed cats would not have gone for the upper neck because if they struck the cervical vertebrae it could snap one of their sabers. Instead, they would aim for the lower neck or throat. After the animal died, the sabers may then have been used to tear or slice muscle and fat.

Other researchers say the deadly sabers may have been used to severely wound large prey like the giant ground sloth or mastodon by attacking the soft underbelly, ripping it open, and then following the animal until it bled to death. A few even think saber-toothed cats fed strictly on carrion because their sabers were so fragile. Breaking one meant the animal could starve to death if it relied on hunting with the blades.

What Happened to the Saber-toothed Cats?

Because saber-toothed cats were so highly adaptive to large game, it's thought that the big cats died out as their prey became extinct. The saber was simply not as effective on smaller game, nor, perhaps, were the cats quick and agile enough to compete with smaller predators specialized in smaller game. Although early man may not have directly hunted saber-toothed cats into extinction, the effect would be the same if he helped wipe out their food source—mammoths, mastodons, and sloths.

Author's cat, Inspector Clueso, resting on a mammoth tooth and dreaming of a former life as a sabercat when he could easily conquer such beasts as a mammoth. Photo by author.

Two moods of the genus *Puma,* known as the panther, puma, cougar, or mountain lion. Its fossil record dates back to about 500,000 years on the American continent. Beyond that, some reason that it is most closely related to the cheetah and to the American cheetahlike cats placed in the genus *Miracinonyx.* Tom, shown here, is a resident of the Babcock Ranch in Charlotte County. Photos by author.

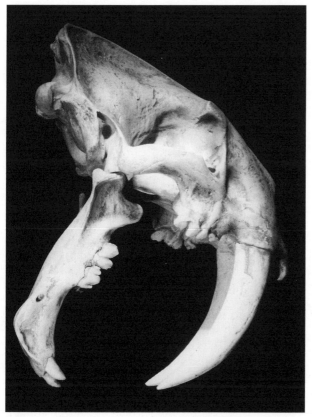

Rancho La Brea sabercat skull cast. Photo by Robin Brown.

Sign in the Everglades. There are fewer than 50 Florida panthers remaining in the wild. Most are found on Big Cypress Preserve in the Everglades. Photo by author.

1 2

When Tanks Had Legs

Armadillos and Glyptodonts

It was well after dark as the young couple made their way home along a narrow stretch of back-country road that snaked its way through a dense pine forest. Rounding a corner at 55 miles per hour, they didn't see the armadillo until it was too late. Instinctively, the strange-looking mammal bucked at the last second, flipping the car on impact.

Wait a second. Did you say "*flipping* the car"? Okay, so the last paragraph was fictional. But if the *Holmesina*—a giant armadillo standing three and a half feet tall and weighing 600 pounds—had survived through Pleistocene extinctions about 10,000 years ago, the scene just described might very well have been real.

Coming to America

Like sloths and anteaters, armadillos belong to the order Edentata, which means "lacking teeth." Early edentates may have been toothless, but somewhere along the line strange-shaped chewing pegs began to show up— although they lacked enamel. The nine-banded armadillo here in Florida eats termites, ants, worms, small snakes, and carrion. But it's doubtful such a diet could keep a 600-pound armadillo happy. More than likely, its eating habits included some vegetation.

It has been 50 million years since these South American mammals—the only ones with true shells—started down the winding road of evolution. As long as North and South America were separated by oceans, armadillos were relatively safe in their isolated world. Once a land bridge formed between the two continents in the late Pliocene epoch about two Ma, large saber-toothed cats begin to migrate southward, while the armadillos headed north. Eventually they would get together over dinner.

Two families made the North American pilgrimage: the enormous Glyptodontidae (which weighed up to two tons and were not true armadillos) and Dasypodidae, which included the *Holmesina; Dasypus bellus* (slightly larger than today's nine-banded armadillos); and all modern armadillos. The Latin taxonomic ending *dae* means "family."

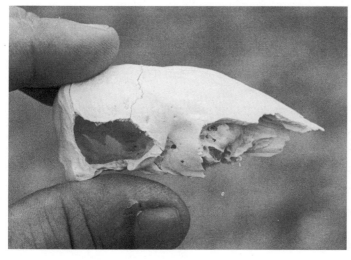

Skull of modern nine-banded armadillo (*Dasypus novemcinctus*). Photo by author.

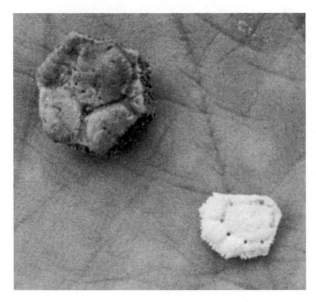

Modern nine-banded armadillo (*Dasypus novemcinctus*) and prehistoric *Dasypus bellus* scutes. Photo by author.

While *Holmesina* belongs to the family Dasypodidae, it also belongs to the subfamily Pampatheriinae. All modern armadillos, including the extinct *Dasypus bellus,* belong to the subfamily Dasypodinae. (*Nae* is the Latin taxonomic ending for subfamily.)

Although their biggest enemy today is the automobile, giant armadillos and glyptodonts of yester-epoch faced much craftier prey in saber-toothed cats and dire wolf packs. But with bony armor up to a half inch thick on the giant armadillo and two inches thick on the glyptodont, leaping onto the slow-moving creatures was probably a great lesson in futility. To make a kill, large predators—including man—would have to find some way to get to the vulnerable underbelly.

Like turtles, glyptodonts lugged around a rigid, nonflexing shell, or carapace. According to Russ McCarty, senior preparator for the Florida Museum of Natural History, armadillos, including the extinct giant Pampatheres (a member of Pampatheriinae), had flexing, movable scutes, which allowed some of them to roll into protective positions.

"The big armadillos may have lost some of their flexibility, but surely retained this ability to some degree as seen from the imbricating (movable) and nonimbricating (immovable) scutes, which we find in association with their fossil remains," says McCarty. "Critters as large as glypts were probably eating more than bugs, invert stuff, and the occasional bit of carrion. They may have been processing plant material too.

"The same can be said for giant armadillos," he continues. "Someone here at the museum suggested the perhaps not-so-far-out idea that the giant armadillos may have been 'coprophages,' eating sloth dung, among other things, since their skeletons have been found in caves out west where thick deposits of sloth dung have been found."

The two edentate cousins, glyptodonts and giant armadillos, coexisted for hundreds of thousands of years throughout most of the Pleistocene epoch (1.81 Ma to 10,000 years B.P.). Glyptodonts were probably already extinct by the time the first humans arrived in Florida some 12,200 years ago, while giant armadillos stuck around to help close out the epoch. Bones found in Hornsby Springs in Alachua County in the 1960s or 1970s were radiocarbon dated at 9,884 years B.P. This is the most recent date known for giant armadillos.

These strange creatures were wiped out by the same mysterious circumstances that forced into extinction saber-toothed cats, mammoths, mastodons, sloths, and other prehistoric beasts. Most researchers blame climatic conditions for reducing the food supply and habitat for the larger herbivores.

Extreme cold weather and drought may have destroyed Florida's lush tropical forests they depended on for food and shelter. Less food and shelter may have driven them to congregate in smaller areas, which would make them easier to hunt by man and the big cats. Once the herbivores were gone, it was only a matter of time before their predators—if they were unable to adapt to the change—followed.

All in the Family

Today, there are some 20 species of armadillos in the world, but only one in the United States. The nine-banded *Dasypus novemcinctus* began to make a comeback in the 1850s after a 10,000-year hiatus. It moved from south to north again, crossing the Rio Grande and entering Texas. It's found as far west as New Mexico and as far southeast as Florida. Because armadillos have no way to store fat, cold weather keeps them from spreading too far north.

Although the nine-banded armadillo is the most numerous, some of the other species share the title for the most unusual. The three-banded armadillo (*Tolypeutes truncatus*) is the only one that can actually roll itself into a ball; the pink fairy armadillo (*Chlamyphorus truncatus*) has a shell attached to the spine and a shovel-like tail for burrowing.

Giant Armadillo Skull Found

The skull of a giant armadillo was found by Eric Taylor, secretary for the Florida Paleontological Society, and Adam Black, a biological illustrator. Russ McCarty pieced together the skull.

"We recovered it from one of the Haile Quarry sites," says McCarty. It is the larger, late Pleistocene species, *Holmesina septentrionalis.*" According to McCarty, the specimen is a juvenile, as evidenced by the unfused epiphyses (growth plate of cartilage instead of bone) on the limb bone. The skull is about 13 inches long.

"The site is probably latest Pleistocene," he says. "It appears that the armadillo fell into a small sinkhole that had little side caverns off to the sides. These little minicaves might have been dens for large predators. In one of them we found a baby dire wolf skull along with the bones of many rabbits."

McCarty says that the Florida Natural History Museum does not have a complete skeleton of an ancient armadillo, but it does have skulls of the small and large species.

"In the [scientific] literature, there are probably five or six giant armadillos mentioned over the last 40 years." he says. "However, more recent researchers such as Gary Morgan and Richard Hulbert have boiled this alphabet soup down to probably just two common types of giant armadillos: the late Pleistocene and early Pleistocene species, *Holmesina floridanus,* which was smaller; and the larger, late Pleistocene species, *Holmesina septentrionalis.*

"There may be another species floating around, but if so, there is not much fossil evidence. All in all, the giant armadillos are not well known, nor have they been written about in depth."

Modern "dillo" Facts

- Armadillos always give birth to four youngsters—all the same sex.
- Armadillos are used in leprosy research because their body temperatures are low enough for them to contract the most virulent form of the disease.
- A stressed-out pregnant female armadillo can actually delay the birth of her young for up to two years (so be nice to the females in particular).
- Although they don't look much like Olympic material, armadillos are strong swimmers. Or, if they prefer, they can cross a pond or creek by walking along the bottom.

Over a hundred glyptodont scutes from one site in DeSoto County creek. There may have been more than 2,000 of these scutes protecting the two-ton animal. Note apple on top for scale. Photo by author.

Glyptodont scute. Photo by Rob Neuhauser.

1 3

Chasing Spirits

The Florida Bison's 500,000-Year Journey

I find their ghosts everywhere, poking out of the steep banks of the Caloosahatchee River in Fort Myers, wrapped in a clump of black dirt left behind in a Polk County phosphate mine, resting on the watery floor of the Gulf of Mexico, 500 yards offshore at Venice Beach. Sometimes it's a tooth, other times a toe bone, a limb bone, or a vertebra. Every time I pick up a piece of a prehistoric bison, I feel as if I'm holding a moment in time, like an ancient three-dimensional photograph.

Judging by how often I find their remains and in how many different Florida locations, I wonder if they were as prolific as today's American bison (*Bison bison*) were in the early 1800s, grazing in great numbers across the peninsula's late Pleistocene grassy savannas. The ancient bison—like their contemporaries—were powerful, lumbering herbivores, although still vulnerable to the crafty predators of their day. No doubt they were hunted by every beast from American lions to 300-pound sabercats, bone-crushing dogs, dire wolves, and eventually Paleo man.

Bison herd approaching the feeding troughs, Babcock Ranch, Charlotte County. Photo by author.

Looking at a tooth in my hand, I can't help but wonder about our state's environment of 10,000, 100,000, or 500,000 years ago, which is as far back as the bison fossil record goes here. If it's true that Florida has been dry land, then ocean, then dry land countless times, how many of those times were bison a part of the dry landscape? How many times did the oceans' encroaching waters force them to migrate north again into higher elevations?

How many times did weather patterns change enough to wipe out the grasses they may have dined on? Or did bison adversely affect their food source by their sheer numbers? Were there really a lot of ancient bison here, or are their teeth and bones common finds because they fossilize easily, or because the animals died in suitable areas for fossilization to occur? There is a lot we know about them, but even more that we don't.

Four-legged Immigrants

Among Eurasia's bovids, which include muskoxen, goats, and sheep, the genus *Bison* was the only one to begin populating Pleistocene Florida some 500,000 years ago. Three species of bison evolved here with nearly identical bone structure, except for the horns. The first was *Bison latifrons,* with a distance of up to six feet between the horn points. *Bison antiquus* had shorter horns with less distance between the points, followed by today's *Bison bison,* whose horn measurements are even shorter.

Fossil hunters who compare the bison teeth they find with those of the modern cow *Bos* (brought here from Europe by early settlers) will have a difficult time distinguishing between the two teeth. What you have may be obvious if you pick up a white tooth on the ground in an active cow pasture, but that same tooth in a creek or river may turn dark brown in a year because of the tannin in the water.

Due to the rich mineral content in our waterways, it's possible too that a tooth lost from a cow brought here by the Spaniards in the 1500s may have fossilized enough to fool you. Then again, I have come across a white "bison" tooth in intact white-colored sediments that also contained fragments of mammoth teeth. So color alone doesn't prove the age or species of a tooth.

Cow and calf. Photo by author.

Where the Buffalo Roam . . .

Buffalo Bill really should have been called Bison Bill (or another not-so-nice name if you ask certain Native Americans). That's because we do not have any buffalo native to North America. Our American bison, with its characteristic "hump," has been called a buffalo so often, many people think that's what it is. But the real buffaloes are Asia's water buffalo and Africa's Cape buffalo—distant cousins to the bison.

The American bison has been the largest land mammal in North America since the end of the Pleistocene. At one time, their numbers may have reached 70 million. There are stories of a single herd stretching out on the horizon 25 miles long and 10 miles wide. It was not unheard of in the early days of expansion out west for train engineers to have to wait two days for the bison to cross the tracks before they could proceed.

But by the late 1800s, there were fewer than 1,500 bison left; most of them had been slaughtered senselessly. Today, however, there are approximately 200,000 of them roaming North America again, mostly in private herds. Media mogul Ted Turner has the largest private herd, numbering in excess of 5,700. The three subspecies we have today are the plains bison, wood bison, and European wisent.

A Bison at Home

A few years ago when I was the operations manager for the nature tours at the 90,000-acre Babcock Ranch in Charlotte County, I had under my care about 38 head of bison. Occasionally, a calf would get sick and would need special attention. Twice I had the unenviable job of separating one from its mother and the rest of the herd.

In one instance, my co-worker and I had to pick up a calf that appeared to have great difficulty walking. Our plan was to drive into the bison pasture with an old pickup truck and try to wedge it between Mom and her baby, then scoop up the calf, and off we'd go. It worked better than we expected. As we approached the pair, Mom trotted away from the youngster while my co-worker and I leaped out of the truck and ran toward the calf.

The American bison's (*Bison bison*) hump is just an extension of the spine. Photo by author.

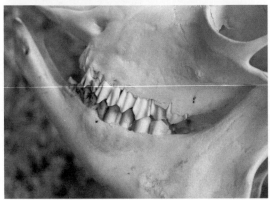

When one of the American bison (*Bison bison*) yearlings died at Babcock Ranch, the author moved it to a field to decompose for about a year. Later, the bones were turned over to Ray Seguin of Fort Myers, who, with the assistance of Robin Brown, reassembled the skeleton. Photos by author.

It was at this point that Murphy's Law came into play. The calf suddenly dipped into its reserves of strength, agility, and speed and darted off, with us running and slipping and falling in hot pursuit. Meanwhile, Mom, who appeared to have abandoned her calf, had actually trotted over to the rest of the herd snorting loudly. In seconds, the entire group had worked itself into a frenzy and was heading our way to intercede on the calf's behalf. We barely got back to the truck before they reached us.

A few days later we were able to catch the calf and take it home. But by then it was too late. It only lived a few days.

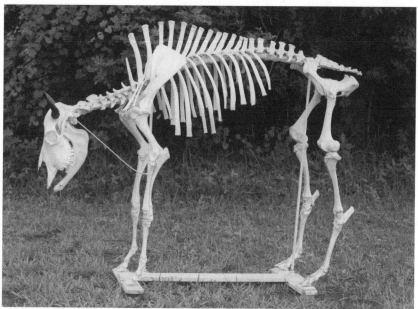

Complete skeleton of the American bison (*Bison bison*) yearling reassembled by Ray Seguin and Robin Brown. Photo by author.

American bison (*Bison bison*) bull, Babcock Ranch. Photo by author.

I learned a lot during the short time I was in charge of these bison. I never missed a chance to observe their behavior, individually and collectively. I would often spend several hours after work just watching them.

One old bull in particular held my attention. He was the undisputed boss and had his way with all the cows. None of the other males would ever challenge him.

But one day I noticed a younger bull face off against the older bull, and I thought, oh boy, this youngster's about to get his first real ass whuppin'. Sure enough, the older, heavier bull knocked the younger one on his side, taking out a barbed-wire fence in the process.

But this defeat did not seem to dampen the younger bull's resolve. Over the next six months the challenges continued. At first the younger bull walked away after his first loss of the day. But then I noticed him come back for a second beating within 10 minutes of the first, then gradually a third, and so on.

Eventually, he wore down the older bull, who could easily win in one round, sometimes two, but just couldn't go the distance.

Once the younger bull became boss, he wouldn't allow the older bull to come anywhere near the rest of the herd. Instead, I would often see him standing alone off to one side of the 50-acre pasture. I know in his own way he had to realize that his day had come and gone, and it was time for younger blood to take over.

It was sad for me to see the whole affair unfold, but fascinating at the same time. I couldn't feel too sorry for the older bull, though, for he had probably used the same tactics to win his position of power in the first place.

Bison Bits

- A full-grown male bison can weigh more than 2,000 pounds. Imagine the migration paths millions of these animals would leave as they traveled from one area to the next, grazing. Settlers referred to these paths as a "trace" and found them ideal for wagon roads. Today, many of our modern highways follow the path of a bison trace.

- Bison horns, unlike deer and elk antlers, are made of a substance similar to hair. Horns are slow growing and are permanent. They are grown in yearly "rings" which signify an animal's age.
- Although they may look fat and lazy, bison can actually run as fast as 35 miles per hour—three times faster than a human.
- Bison have been known to clear a six-foot fence or knock it down—whichever they choose.

11,000-Year-Old Bison Kill Site

In the summer of 1982, a *Bison antiquus* skull was found in the Wacissa River. Known as the Alexon Bison site, it became one of many late Pleistocene sites suggesting that Paleo-Indians occupied the lower Aucilla River and its tributary, the Wacissa.

"The bison with the 'point' in its skull was found by amateur collector Roger Alexon in the Wacissa River," says Russ McCarty, senior preparator for the Florida Museum of Natural History. "The radiocarbon date of 11,000 years plus came not from the skull but from an associated limb bone found nearby.

"The point penetrates the top of the skull between the horns, a little right of the midline suture. It goes into a sinus cavity in the skull and would not have hit the bison's brain. Since there is no evidence of bone growth or regeneration around the stone point, we know that the animal died at the time it received this wound in its head. However, it did not die from this wound, but from others received at the same time, to other parts of the body. It is probably one of the best direct associations of humans and extinct animals in the new world."

Herd, Babcock Ranch. Photo by author.

Bison latifrons horn cores. The distance between points is 52 inches.
Photo by Robin Brown.

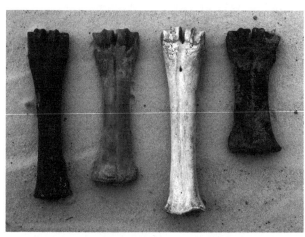

Can you tell which of these specimens are cow cannon bones and which are from *Bison antiquus*? (Answer: They're all from modern cows.) Photo by Sunny Sung.

14

Where on Earth Are They?

Sniffing Around for Old Bones

You've pumped enough gas in your car to cross the Sahara Desert, and it's loaded with more Oreos and sodas than most elementary school lunchrooms. Your road map is taped to the dash, and you're ready for some serious fossil hunting. So where do you go?

Since I don't know where you live, I can only tell you what works well for me. Where I live, it doesn't matter if I head north, south, east, or west. I know I'm bound to come across enough fossils to be accused of robbing a museum—*if* I know where to look. That's because Florida has a fossil record as rich in bones as the U.S. Treasury Department is in gold bars and green-faced presidents.

I live in an area of Lee County known as Lehigh Acres. It's 35 feet above sea level, whereas other parts of the county average about 8 to 10 feet above sea level. That means that during glacial stages of melting ice on the poles, Lehigh Acres was probably an island—some of the only high ground for quite a few miles.

MARISA '18

Since I've had a lot of luck finding old bones in creeks and rivers, that's where I focus my searches. Finding a nice, dry pit or quarry is even better, but most are privately operated and the owners don't want to run the risk of getting sued should you accidentally trip over a mammoth tooth. So don't count on getting in.

The first thing I do is spread out my wrinkled map, brush off the cookie crumbs, and highlight every body of water within a 40-mile radius. I didn't become certified as a scuba diver until I had been fossiling for over a year, so I looked initially for shallow creeks or those with banks artificially created by dredge material.

I started with the Caloosahatchee River because I lived near it when I first caught the bone bug. Borrowing a canoe, I entered the river at public boat ramps and easy access points, searching for brown and black pebbly-looking material mixed in with the white sand. From talking to people with experience in this field, I had learned that shark teeth and other fossils would most likely be in that kind of sediment.

I also looked for white, brown, and nearly black bone exposed in areas where the U.S. Army Corps of Engineers had cut through the natural banks while dredging the river. (Later, I learned that land animal fossils can also be found in the rich, black soil laid down on top of freshwater shells.)

I did well in the Caloosahatchee River, or so it seemed, until I began to venture out into other creeks and rivers and found out that there was a wealth of material just about everywhere. Since the Peace River had a reputation for easy fossil pickings, I grabbed my snorkel gear one day and set out in that direction. Unfortunately, I showed up during the height of the rainy season to find the water high, murky, and fast flowing.

I returned during the dry season and began searching in two to three feet of water. At first, all I could see was sand interspersed with large pebbles. Then a fragment of black turtle shell caught my attention. I fanned the sand lightly with my hand and made my way down to a hard sandstone bottom. On top of this sandstone were more fossils.

While I won't get spiritual with you on the best ways to pinpoint a fossil hot spot, there is something to be said for "feeling" out a location. Common sense may tell you your best bet is to start searching right after a bend in a creek because fossils may have been washed out and pushed slightly downstream. But I have found them in the most unlikely places.

A DeSoto County creek during the summer rainy season with a depth of about eight feet. The same creek in the winter dry season may only be two feet deep. Photo by Marisa Renz.

During the winter dry season, Florida creeks are shallow, making it easier to hunt fossils. But be careful. This particular creek in Charlotte County is home to many alligators. Photo by author.

The same creeks during the summer rainy season may be flooded, making the search more difficult, except with scuba gear. Photo by author.

Sometimes they are at the end of a long straightaway. Sometimes they are at the beginning. Sometimes they are in the middle of a creek or river, and sometimes they are on the edges. There are even places where you'll find fossils mixed in with the asphalt roadbeds such as the one just to the right of the Peace River boat ramp in Arcadia. There are far too many variables involved to come up with a law of fossil locales.

Consider the following example: A mammoth dies a million years ago at the edge of a freshwater marsh. Its carcass is scattered 500 feet in every direction by scavengers. Part of the skeleton gets covered up by the mud at the bottom of the marsh. Ten thousand years later, a river changes its course and cuts through the marsh, breaking the remaining parts of the skeleton into smaller pieces and further scattering the bones. A hundred thousand years later, a glacial cycle forces the oceans to rise. The resulting tidal action breaks much of the bone into tiny, indistinguishable fragments.

I don't limit my opportunities by remaining in one spot too long. If I don't see any healthy sign of fossils within two or three minutes, it's on to another area. When I do finally locate a spot, I don't just start picking up bones. This is very important to me because I don't want to miss anything. I want to get a feel for the way the bones are arranged on the bottom. Is there a possibility of an entire animal here? Where were the bones before? Did they wash out of the bottom or the bank?

Ancient shells can also be found in Florida's creeks and rivers. This whelk was uncovered along the banks of the Caloosahatchee River in Hendry County. Photo by author.

The fossil horse tooth in the lower right corner shows how well some fossils may blend in with their surroundings. Photo by author.

Sinkholes do contain fossils, but diving is usually the only way to check them out. Forget it, unless you're a veteran to the dangerous conditions they can present. "Big Dismal" sinkhole, shown here, is in Leon County. Photo by Robin Brown.

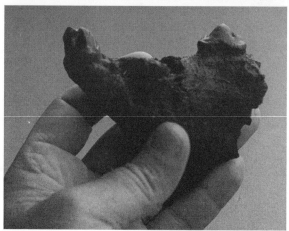

A tooth from this jaguar jaw was all that was sticking out of the Caloosahatchee River bank. Photo by author.

I start by backing myself downstream to where the hot spot appears to begin. Then, with mask and snorkel, I fan through the surface material to see how deep the fossils are buried. Gradually, I work my way up to where the hot spot ends.

Getting a little more sophisticated with searching methods, some fossilers have obtained U.S. Geological Survey topographical maps (which show elevations) to pinpoint the most likely spots to dig in. To some degree, this is a sensible way to search. If you know the current sea level of the land in your area, and how the land formations are supposed to be laid out, finding the good stuff should be a piece of cake. But it's not. Consider that Florida's sediments were not laid down like layers of a cake. They're more like the ups and downs of a roller coaster.

Here, you may go down 10 feet to find sediments 100,000 years old. A few feet away at the same depth might take you back a million years. The 10-million-year-old dugong I found was only 4 feet below the surface. Yet 5-million-year-old shark teeth are often found in pits over 40 feet deep.

Don't be fooled into thinking that because you found a horse tooth in a formation one million years old, the tooth is necessarily that age. Here's why: Imagine a horse dying a million years ago. Part of its carcass gets covered up on dry ground, another part gets dragged by an alligator into a nearby river with a tooth lying on the bank and more teeth getting scattered 10 feet under the river's surface. Each part of that animal could conceivably settle into a different formation because of the way water— whether it's a river or the ocean—can wash things around and mix up bones and teeth. So if you really need to know how old a fossil is, it's better to rely on more than one method of dating.

Over the last 100 years alone, elevations have changed significantly in many areas because of human intervention. Man often fills in low-lying areas (sometimes with older sediments taken from somewhere else), digs out other areas, redirects waterways, or slows them down considerably. All these conditions will have some effect on what you're going to find.

To find fossils in many creeks or rivers, I usually look for the bone fragment clues I mentioned earlier. Sometimes creeks with a lot of old-growth native vegetation along the banks are a good indication that the waterway may not have changed much over the last few hundred years. Many creeks were swamps or marshes for thousands of years before assuming their present form. Prehistoric animals often gathered around wetlands because they needed the water to survive. Naturally, many of them would also die near water.

Some canals are cut through higher ground where wetlands may not have existed. So you may find it harder to find fossils there. Other canals may run directly through an ancient marsh, exposing finds of a lifetime. You just never know until you get out there and look. Sometimes the best teacher is trial and error.

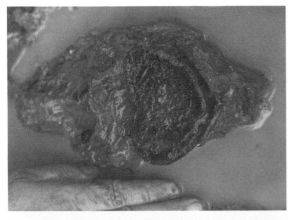

Dugong vertebra along the banks of the Peace River in Hardee County. Photo by author.

Whale vertebra on river bottom in Lee County. Don't pick it up until you've searched around it to see how much of the animal is present. In this case, an entire 45-foot whale skeleton and baby 9-footer were gradually uncovered. Photo by Robin Brown.

This mammoth tooth blended in so well, it was difficult to spot in the banks of the Caloosahatchee River. Photo by author.

But once out of the bank and cleaned up, it was more easily recognizable as that of a mammoth, Caloosahatchee River, Lee County. Photo by author.

A two-ton glyptodont (armadillo) may have died here, but all that remains are two of its 2,000-plus scutes. Photo by author.

Extremely fragile ribs (species unknown), buried under five feet of water and a foot of well-packed sand, Peace River, Hardee County. Photo by author.

15

Hunting in Style

How You Look Is as Important as Where You Look

Most people will tell you that to get the really good stuff, you need a little luck and a lot of patience. To a certain degree, they're right. But what you need more than anything is to know what you're looking for and how to look for it. What good is persistence if you're looking in the wrong area? Or if you're hunting along a creek bottom with a mask and snorkel when you should be probing the muck of the creek bank with your fingertips? Here are some methods I use:

Robbing the Right Bank

For about six months, I snorkeled along the bottoms of shallow creeks and rivers, picking up a bone here and a bone there. I was so grateful just to find something—anything—that I didn't give the hows and whys a whole lot of thought. One day I stopped long enough to ask myself, "Why are these bones here and not behind me a hundred feet? Why had they shown them-

A smidgen of skill, a little luck, and a heckuva lot of perseverance add up to afternoons like this. Finds include a mastodon tooth, several large "Meg" teeth, a mammoth vertebra, archaic point, and horse teeth. Photo by author.

selves after a million years of hiding? Were they washed out of the creek bottom or the creek bank? And was the camel toe bone I uncovered really an isolated find, or was the rest of the animal nearby?"

What really woke me up to using some kind of methodology in fossiling was when I returned to a particular creek the second year and found fossils resting on top of a hard limestone clay that weren't there the previous year. I knew they couldn't have washed up from the bottom in one rainy season. Therefore—at least in this particular case—the creek's flow must have flushed them out of the bank.

I started probing around in the muddy bank with my fingers, working them underneath some old-growth oak trees. It wasn't long before I turned up a fossilized turtle shell, then a sea cow rib fragment, then an ancient horse tooth. Not only did this method double my chance of finding fossils, it offered me a place (the banks) to hunt when the water was too deep or murky for snorkeling.

I also looked closely at the roots of some of the cabbage palms along the banks of this creek. I was surprised to find fossils sticking out of the root ball—as if the roots had pushed them out of the bank. As a result of this

The author working his fingers through the mud to the clay bottom where the fossils are buried. Photo by Marisa Renz.

method, I have a nice alligator jaw in my home display with small feeler roots protruding out of the tooth sockets.

When you notice a hard creek or river bottom, keep in mind that it may have originated several feet up the bank, but the flow of water has worn it down. Oftentimes, I find bank fossils that are lying on the original hard clay bottom, some of them above the present-day waterline. I work my fingers through the softer sediments until I hit that clay bottom. Then I feel around until I make contact with bone or clay. If I hit bone, I set up camp. If not, I move on.

Another method I use is to look for gravelly areas in the banks, not just in the middle of streambeds. Wading along parts of the Peace River, for example, I noticed gravel 15 feet above me in the bank. Upon closer inspection, I found shark teeth, horse and bison teeth, dugong ribs, and other bones.

Snorkeling Is for Shallow Minds

Under the right conditions, nothing compares to snorkeling. When the water is shallow and clear, you can slip your entire body under the surface and enter a world completely different from the one above the surface. There could be a busy highway in the background or kids laughing and

Members of the Tampa Bay Fossil Club screen-wash in the shallows of the Peace River. Photo by author.

Frank and Betty Kocsis searching for the ever-elusive extinct giant white. Peace River. Photo by author.

playing nearby. You won't hear them. Snorkeling takes you back in time physically as well as mentally. Without a lot of distractions, it's easier to focus your attention on finding a record of the past.

When I snorkel in a creek or river, I'm usually in two or three feet of water. I look for rocky or gravelly areas that might also contain bones and teeth. If I notice a few bones here and there on the sandy bottom, I'll gently fan away the sand with my hand to see if there are any fossils farther down. Quite often there are.

My best finds have come about while snorkeling. The giant ground sloth I uncovered was in two feet of water, the saber-toothed cat and jaguar remains were shallow-water finds, as were entire mammoth teeth and my wife's five-and-a-half-inch extinct giant white shark tooth. The list goes on and on.

With snorkeling, you can travel lighter than with scuba gear, and cover more water—because you never run out of air. The best time to snorkel in southwest Florida, where I live, is between November and May, which is the dry season. In northern Florida, you may encounter the opposite conditions during this time.

Scuba for an In-depth Look

There's no question that diving will take you into the deeper holes and improve your odds for finding larger fossils. That hasn't been true for me, but only because I have done more shallow-water snorkeling than diving. For the most part, shallow creeks and rivers—especially those with a strong flow—tend to break bones up as they're pushed along the bottom by water and debris. But in deeper holes, the current is much weaker, increasing the odds that larger bones will remain intact.

Most of Florida's waterways are reddish brown because of the tannin leaching into the water. The deeper the water, the darker it gets, making fossil hunting without a dive light difficult. In many places where I dive, several feet of sand or muck may cover the fossils. Without a strong flow, it's easy to stir up the bottom, making visibility impossible, even with a light.

I sometimes carry along an aluminum tent pole and use it as a probe, gently poking it through mucky bottoms until I hear that familiar "clink, clink" sound of fossilized bone. Then I reach down through the muck to pull up whatever is there—being careful not to stir things up too much. I also don't wear my fins in water with a weak flow so that they don't stir up the bottom.

As with any endeavor, there is an art to being a good bonesmith. Decide what you want and know which tools you will need for the job. Develop a method that works best for you. Then practice persistence.

Dad and daughter can spend time together. Photo by author.

From 9 to 90, it can be as easy as . . . well, picking up bones. Photo by author.

One job you can sit down on. Photo by author.

Some sites are more productive than others. These are "Meg" teeth from the Peace River in Hardee County. Photo by author.

This alligator jaw was found in the roots of a cabbage palm tree along the banks of a DeSoto County creek. Look closely and you can see feeler roots weaving through the jaw. Photo by author.

Along the Caloosa-hatchee River in Hendry County, one of the ways to search is to look for material washed out of the bank by the waves of passing boats. Photo by author.

The author's friend Jim Farrell with an afternoon's worth of giant tortoise shell fragments from one small site. He was working with his hands in the bank behind the bones. Photo by author.

What aching back?!
Photo by author.

Sifting out the un-
wanted material.
Photo by author.

A shovel full of . . . fossils? Photo by author.

Screening out the unwanted material.
Photo by author.

How you look is as important as where you
look. Photo by Marisa Renz.

Diving in five feet of water
allows you to gently fan
through sand on the bot-
tom and beats bobbing up
to the surface every 20 seconds. George Diaz, Peace
River, Hardee County.
Photo by author.

By snorkeling, you can travel light and cover a lot of territory. Photo by Marisa Renz.

If you look closely, you can see tiny feeler roots from a tree running through part of this mammoth vertebra. Examine riverbanks that have steep walls for fossils just above the shell line in dark sediments. Caloosahatchee River, Lee County. Photo by author.

The fossilized alligator jaw shown earlier in this chapter was found in the roots of the cabbage palm on left. DeSoto County stream. Photo by author.

16

Whatizit?

Prehistoric Bison or the Farmer's Lost Cow?

The male voice on my phone's answering machine sounded urgent. "I've found the jaw of a saber-toothed tiger," he exclaimed. "Can you come over and take a look at it?" When I returned his call, I asked him to describe what he had found. His description of the teeth did sort of fit the saber-toothed cat—a row of wicked-looking incisors with two menacing fangs. I said I would be right over.

As soon as I saw the jaw, I felt like an idiot for not asking him more questions before I drove all the way across town to view the mandible of a modern feral hog. But I let his enthusiasm sway me. I should have asked precisely where he had found it and its color. It was lying on the ground in an open field and was white.

Color by itself does not prove a bone's age. White fossilized bones are the norm in some phosphate pits; they're also the color of a modern cow skeleton. Dark brown or black fossilized bones are most common in creeks

MARISA '47

and rivers. But modern bones exposed to river water can turn brown in a matter of months. They can also turn a dirty brown when buried in the ground.

The weight of a fossil doesn't prove anything either. A cow leg bone can wash into a river and absorb enough minerals in a hundred years to become partially fossilized and slightly heavier. It may actually weigh more than a million-year-old bison leg bone the same size that was buried in sediments containing fewer minerals.

To identify what you have found, compare your find with the fossils pictured in the "Prehistoric Portraits" section of this book or with the

By the time you've read this book, you should be able to identify each of these fossils. Want to try it now? Photo by Robin Brown.

photographs in other books listed in the bibliography. To detect whether a bone is fossilized or not, here are some suggestions:

1. Light a match to it; if it smells like burning human hair, it still contains protein and is modern.
2. Tap it lightly with a screwdriver or other metal object: if it's fossilized, it will probably sound like china.
3. Determine the epoch in which the animal lived.
4. Ascertain the age of the sediments surrounding the fossil.

Forget about radiocarbon dating. It is expensive, and part of the bone may have to be destroyed for the test. Plus, its maximum reach into the past is a little over 50,000 years, just the most recent part of the Pleistocene epoch. Other methods of radioactive dating reach farther back but require special minerals seldom found in Florida specimens.

There are approximately 214 bones in most mammals. They are not all identical in shape from species to species, but many of them are similar enough to get a rough idea of the particular body part you are trying to identify. For instance, look at some of the toe bones pictured in this chapter. If they are land animals and walk on all fours, you should see a common shape and density to them. The same goes for their leg bones, ankle bones, sockets, and even their teeth, depending on diet similarities.

Some modern bones so closely resemble fossilized ones that it's tough to tell how old a bone really is. Take the prehistoric bison. Its teeth look much the same as those of a modern cow. So do some of its leg bones, only they are slightly thicker. It's sometimes difficult, too, to tell whether you have found the fossilized tooth of an ancient camel, deer, or llama. But there are differences under close examination.

If you want to get serious, locate a cleaned-up skeleton or two of a dog, opossum, sheep, or deer. Even two such examples will quickly give you the basis for comparison and will lead toward sound identification. Having these three-dimensional objects also makes it easier to understand the two-dimensional pictures in a book like this.

Giant tortoise dermal armor, also known as a heinie binder. Photo by author.

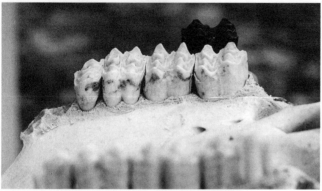

Cow jaw and teeth with bison tooth for comparison. Photo by author.

Cow bones scattered in a field. Some scientists estimate that the odds are about a million to one that a bone will ever become fossilized. Photo by author.

Water-worn dugong ribs and other bones shaped like rocks. Photo by Robin Brown.

Petrified wood from the Peace River, Hardee County. Photo by author.

A prehistoric peace sign? Turtle shell fragment, underbelly just behind head. Photo by Sunny Sung.

Fish vertebrae come in all sizes, shapes, and colors. Photo by author.

PREHISTORIC PORTRAITS

Identifying Your Finds

Alligators
Order: Crocodillia; family: Alligatoridae

Alligator tooth; species: *Alligator mississippiensis;* epoch: Pleistocene; location: Prairie Creek; county: DeSoto; measurements: 2 inches long x ⅝ inch thick. Photo by Sunny Sung.

Alligator mandible; species: *Alligator mississippiensis;* epoch: Pleistocene; location: Joshua Creek; county: DeSoto; measurements: 5 inches long x 2 inches deep. Photo by Sunny Sung.

Alligator scutes (osteoderms); species: *Alligator mississippiensis;* epoch: Pleistocene; location: Joshua Creek; county: DeSoto; measurements: 4 inches x 3¾ inches. Light-colored one is fossilized but was found in a white-colored clay. Photo by Sunny Sung.

Alligator vertebrae; species: *Alligator mississippiensis;* epoch: Pleistocene; location: Imperial River; county: Lee; measurements: the largest one is 3 inches wide x 2½ inches high x 2¾ inches long. Photo by Sunny Sung.

Alligator coprolite; species: *Alligator mississippiensis;* epoch: Pleistocene; location: Peace River; county: Hardee; measurements: 5 inches long. Photo by Sunny Sung.

Armadillos
Order: Edentata; family: Dasypodidae

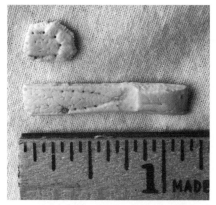

Nine-banded armadillo scutes (modern); species: *Dasypus novemcinctus;* epoch: Holocene; location: open field; county: DeSoto; measurements: see scale. Photo by Sunny Sung.

Small armadillo scutes; species: *Dasypus bellus;* epoch: Pleistocene; location: Prairie Creek; county: DeSoto; measurements: see scale. Photo by Sunny Sung.

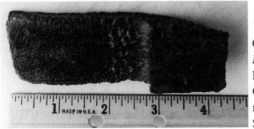

Giant armadillo scute; species: *Holmesina septentrionalis;* epoch: Pleistocene; location: Charlie Creek; county: DeSoto; measurements: see scale. Photo by Sunny Sung.

Giant armadillo scutes; species: *Holmesina septentrionalis;* epoch: Pleistocene; location: Charlie Creek; county: DeSoto; measurements: long one is 4½ inches long x 1¼ inches wide. Photo by Sunny Sung.

Armadillos (not a true armadillo)
Order: Edentata; family: Glyptodontidae

Glyptodont scute; species: *Glyptotherium floridanum;* epoch: Pleistocene; location: Peace River; county: DeSoto; measurements: 2 inches long x 2 inches wide x ⅝ inch thick. Photo by Sunny Sung.

Glyptodont scutes; species: *Glyptotherium floridanum;* epoch: Pleistocene; location: Peace River; county: DeSoto; measurements: 2 inches across. Photo by Sunny Sung.

Giant armadillo mandible sections; species: *Holmesina septentrionalis;* epoch: Pleistocene; location: Myakkahatchee Creek; county: Sarasota. Photo by Sunny Sung.

Size comparison of the various armadillo scutes. See previous illustrations for identification and sizes. Photo by Sunny Sung.

Barracuda
Family: Sphyraenidae

Barracuda teeth; genus: *Sphyraena;* epoch: Pleistocene; location: Caloosahatchee River; county: Lee; measurements: ¾ inch long x ⅜ inch wide. Photo by Sunny Sung.

Short-faced bear
Family: Ursidae

Bear incisor; genus: *Arctodus*; epoch: Pleistocene; location: Prairie Creek; county: DeSoto; measurements: 2¾ inches. Photo by Sunny Sung.

Bear molar; genus: *Arctodus*; epoch: Pleistocene; location: Caloosahatchee River; county: Hendry; measurements: 2¾ inches long x ½ inch wide. Photo by Sunny Sung.

Beaver
Family: Castoridae

Giant beaver molar; species: *Castoroides ohioensis*; epoch: Pleistocene; location: Prairie Creek; county: DeSoto; measurements: ½ inch chewing surface x 1 inch deep. Photo by Sunny Sung.

Bison
Family: Bovidae

Bison lower premolar; species: *Bison antiquus*; epoch: Pleistocene; location: Prairie Creek; county: DeSoto; measurements: 1¼ inches long x ¾ inch wide. Photo by Sunny Sung.

Bison upper premolar; species: *Bison antiquus;* epoch: Pleistocene; location: Prairie Creek; county: DeSoto; measurements: 1¼ inches long x ½ inch wide. Photo by Sunny Sung.

Bison upper molar; species: *Bison antiquus;* epoch: Plieistocene; location: Peace River; county: Hardee; measurements: 1¼ inches long x ¾ inch wide. Photo by Sunny Sung.

Bison molar; species: *Bison antiquus;* epoch: Pleistocene; location: Myakkahatchee Creek; county: Sarasota; measurements: 1½ inches long x ⅝ inch wide. Photo by Sunny Sung.

Bison toe bone (phalanx), two views; species: *Bison antiquus;* epoch: Pleistocene; location: Josuah Creek; county: DeSoto; measurements: 3 inches long x 2 inches wide. Photos by author.

Bison ankle bone (astragalus); species: *Bison antiquus;* epoch: Pleistocene; location: Caloosahatchee River; county: Hendry; measurements: 2¼ inches x 3¼ inches. Photo by Sunny Sung.

Camel
Family: Camelidae (means "camel-like," includes llamalike beasts)

Camelid premolar; genus: *Hemiauchenia*; epoch: Pleistocene; location: DeSoto County creek; county: Hardee; measurements: 1⅔ inches long x ¾ inch wide. Photo by Sunny Sung.

Camelid lower molar; genus: *Hemiauchenia*; epoch: Pleistocene; location: Peace River; county: Hardee; measurements: 2 inches wide x 2¼ inches high. Photo by Sunny Sung.

Camelid cannon bone and toe bones; genus: *Hemiauchenia*; epoch: Pleistocene; location: Joshua Creek; county: DeSoto; measurements: 16½ inches (cannon bone) and 4 inches (one of the toe bones). Photo by Sunny Sung.

Capybara
Family: Hydrochoeridae

Capybara molars; species: *Neochoerus pinckneyi*; epoch: Pleistocene; location: Prairie Creek; county: DeSoto; measurements: 1½ inches long x ½ inch wide x ⅝ inch deep. Capybaras are the largest rodents in North America. Photos by Sunny Sung.

Capybara incisor tooth; species: *Neochoerus pinckneyi;* epoch: Pleistocene; location: DeSoto County creek; measurements: 3 inches x 1 inch. Photo by Sunny Sung.

Cats
Sabercats and Jaguars
Family: Felidae

Sabercat mandible with teeth; genus: *Smilodon;* epoch: Pleistocene; location: DeSoto County creek; measurements: 2½ inches long x 1¼ inches deep. Photo by Sunny Sung.

Jaguar maxilla fragment with teeth; species: *Panthera onca;* epoch: Pleistocene; location: Myakkahatchee Creek; county: Sarasota; measurements: 3 inches long x 2 inches wide. Photo by Sunny Sung.

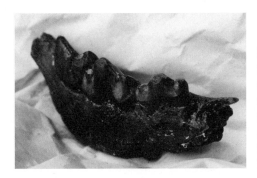

Jaguar mandible fragment with teeth (molar or carnassial tooth is on left; premolars on right); species: *Panthera onca;* epoch: Pleistocene; location: Prairie Creek; county: DeSoto; measurements: 3 inches long x 1 inch deep. Photo by Sunny Sung.

Jaguar skull; species: *Panthera onca;* epoch: Pleistocene; location: Florida Museum of Natural History (FLMNH), Gainesville. Photo by author.

Jaguar tooth; species: *Panthera onca;* epoch: Pleistocene; location: FLMNH, Gainesville. Photo by author.

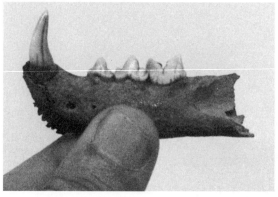

Bobcat mandible; genus: *Lynx;* epoch: Pleistocene; location: FLMNH, Gainesville. Photo by author.

Saber-toothed cat canine tooth; species: *Smilodon gracilis;* epoch: Pleistocene; location: FLMNH, Gainesville. Photo by author.

Saber-toothed cat (also known as false saber-toothed cat); species: *Barbourofelis loveorum;* location: originally Love Bone Bed, Archer; now at FLMNH, Gainesville. Photo by author.

Saber-toothed cat canine tooth; species: *Homotherium (Dinobastis) serum;* location: DeSoto County creek; measurements: 4 inches long. This cat's sabers were not as long as *Smilodon*'s but were broader and more flattened, with a razor-sharp serrated cutting edge on the outside of the bend. Photo by author.

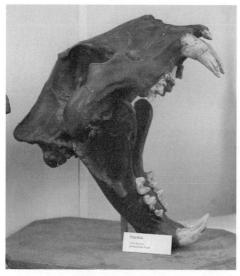

Florida lion; species: *Panthera atrox;* location: originally Ichetucknee River; now at FLMNH, Gainesville. Photo by author.

Earliest sabercat; species: *Smilodon gracilis;* location: originally Leisey shell pit near Tampa Bay, now at FLMNH, Gainesville. Photo by author.

Saber-toothed cat; genus: *Homotherium;* location: originally Haile Quarries, Newberry, now at FLMNH, Gainesville. Photo by author.

Deer
Family: Cervidae

Deer cannon bone and astragalus (ankle bone); genus: *Odocoileus;* epoch: Pleistocene; location: Orange River; county: Lee; measurements: cannon bone is 9 inches long x ¾ inch wide. Photo by Sunny Sung.

Deer mandible; genus: *Odocoileus;* epoch: Pleistocene; location: Joshua Creek; county: DeSoto; measurements: 3½ inches from left to right tooth. Photo by author.

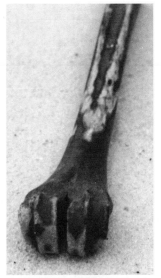

Deer antler and tine; genus: *Odocoileus;* epoch: Pleistocene; location: Orange River; county: Lee; measurements: 5 inches (antler fragment). Photo by Sunny Sung.

Deer cannon bone; genus: *Odocoileus;* epoch: Pleistocene; location: Orange River; county: Lee; measurements: entire bone is 8 inches long. Photo by Sunny Sung.

Dolphin
Suborder: Odontoceti (toothed whales and dolphins)

Dolphin tooth; genus: *Pomatodelphis;* epoch: Miocene; location: Peace River; county: Hardee; measurements: ¾ inch by ½ inch. Photo by Sunny Sung.

Dolphin jaw; genus: unknown; epoch: Miocene/Pliocene; location: Peace River; county: Polk; measurements: 3½ inches long, ½ inch wide. Photo by Sunny Sung.

Dolphin ear bone; genus: *Pomatodelphis;* epoch: Pliocene; location: Caloosahatchee River; county: Hendry; measurements: 1½ inches wide x 1 inch deep. Photo by Sunny Sung.

Dolphin vertebra; genus: *Pomatodelphis;* epoch: Pliocene; location: Caloosahatchee River; county: Hendry; measurements: 2 inches across x 1½ inches thick.

Dugong
Order: Sirenia (sea cows, manatees, and dugongs)
Family: Dugongidae

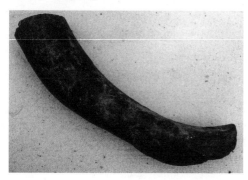

Dugong rib fragment; species: *Metaxytherium floridanum;* epoch: Miocene; location: Peace River; county: Hardee; measurements: between 6 and 8 inches long, up to 2 inches thick. Photo by Sunny Sung.

Dugong vertebra; species: *Metaxytherium floridanum;* epoch: Micocene; location: Peace River shoreline; county: Polk; measurements: 3 inches wide x 1¾ inches thick. Photo by author.

Family: Trichechidae (manatees)

Manatee teeth; genus: *Trichechus;* epoch: Pleistocene; location: Prairie Creek; county: Desoto; measurements: ½ x ½ inch. Photo by author.

Manatee inner ear bone; genus: *Trichechus;* epoch: Pleistocene; location: Prairie Creek; county: DeSoto; measurements: 3 inches long x 2 inches wide. Photo by Sunny Sung.

Eagle ray
Family: Myliobatidae

Eagle ray pavement teeth, articulated and isolated; genus: *Myliobatis;* epoch: Pleistocene; location: Caloosahatchee River; county: Lee; measurements: whole plate 2½ inches long x 2 inches wide. Photo by Sunny Sung.

Eagle ray dermal plates; genus: *Myliobatis;* epoch: Pleistocene; location: Joshua Creek; county: DeSoto; measurements: the one on the right is 2½ inches x 2½ inches. Photo by Sunny Sung.

Eagle ray stinger barbs; genus: *Myliobatis;* epoch: Miocene; location: Peace River; county: Hardee; measurements: Long one is 2½ inches. Photo by Sunny Sung.

Fish—gar
Order: Holostei
Family: Lepisosteidae

Garfish scales; genus: *Lepisosteus;* epoch: Pleistocene; location: Caloosahatchee River; county: Hendry; measurements: Largest one is 1 inch. Photo by Sunny Sung.

Fish—bony
Family: Diodontidae (porcupine fish)

Porcupine fish mouth part; genus: *Diodon;* epoch: Pleistocene; location: Caloosahatchee River; county: Lee; measurements: Larger one is 1½ inches x ½ inch. Photo by Sunny Sung.

Family: Sciaenidae (drum fish)

Drum fish teeth in jaw; species: *Pogonias cromis;* epoch: Pleistocene; location: Myakkahatchee Creek; county: Sarasota; measurements: 2 inches long x 1½ inches wide. Photo by Sunny Sung.

Fish ballast bone or tilly bone; genus: undetermined; epoch: Miocene; location: Myakkahatchee Creek; county: Sarasota; measurements: 1½ inches long x ⅝ inch wide. Photo by Sunny Sung.

Fish nostril cavity; genus: undetermined; epoch: Pleistocene; location: Caloosahatchee River; county: Hendry; measurements: ⅝ inch long x ½ inch wide. Photo by Sunny Sung.

Horse
Family: Equidae

Three-toed horse teeth; genus: *Nannippus;* epoch: Pliocene; location: Prairie Creek; county: DeSoto; measurements: tooth on left is ⅞ inch long x ½ inch wide. Photo by Sunny Sung.

If you look at the chewing surface of an *Equus* (modern-size horse) tooth (left) and the smaller *Nannippus* (three-toed horse) tooth (right), the small tooth has an isolated island—or protocone—at the top of the tooth. While the island is only marked on upper molars, it is a way of separating a juvenile *Equus* tooth from an adult *Nannippus* tooth. The larger tooth does not have a complete island. Photo by Sunny Sung.

Horse teeth (upper molar on top, lower molar on bottom); genus: *Equus;* epoch: Pleistocene; location: Peace River; county: Hardee; measurements: 4⅛ inches long x 1 inch wide (upper tooth). Photo by Sunny Sung.

Comparison of tooth size in *Nannippus* and *Equus.* Photo by Sunny Sung.

Comparison of leg (cannon bone) and foot bone in modern and ancient horses. White bones on left are modern toe bones of an adult horse. At right, from top down, are the hoof core, two toe bones, and the cannon bone from a fossilized adult horse, which is 12 inches long. Photo by Sunny Sung.

Horse sacrum; genus: *Equus;* epoch: Pleistocene; location: Joshua Creek; county: DeSoto; measurements: 6½ inches long x 5½ inches wide (at widest section). Photo by Sunny Sung.

Mammoths
Family: Elephantidae (mammoths and modern elephants)

Mammoth teeth found near each other; genus: *Mammuthus;* epoch: Pleistocene; location: Salt Creek; county: Sarasota; measurements: larger tooth is 7¾ inches long x 3 inches wide x 6 inches deep. Photo by Sunny Sung.

Mammoth lower molar (m2/m3); genus: *Mammuthus;* epoch: Pleistocene; location: shallow creek; county: DeSoto; measurements: 13-inch-long chewing surface x 3¼ inches wide x 5 inches deep. Photo by Sunny Sung.

Mammoth molar tooth (m3); genus: *Mammuthus;* epoch: Pleistocene; location: Prairie Creek; county: DeSoto; measurements: 5½-inch-long chewing surface x 3 inches wide x 10 inches deep. Photo by Sunny Sung.

Mammoth foot bone; species: undetermined; epoch: Pleistocene; location: Caloosahatchee River; county: Lee; measurements: 3 inches long x 2¾ inches wide x 1¼ inches deep. Photo by Sunny Sung.

Mammoth/mastodon tusk—two views; species: undetermined; epoch: Pleistocene; location: Prairie Creek; county: DeSoto; measurements: 3 inches thick. This tusk, possibly from a female or young mammoth, has rings as well as fine raised lines running in different directions. Photos by Sunny Sung.

Mammoth tooth (possibly m3); species: *Mammuthus columbi;* epoch: late Pleistocene; location: Shallow Creek; county: DeSoto; measurements: 10-inch-long chewing surface x 3½ inches wide x 8 inches deep. Photo by Sunny Sung.

Mastodon
Family: Mammutidae

American mastodon tooth cusp (cutaway); genus: *Mammut;* epoch: Pliocene; location: Sante Fe River; county: Gilchrist; measurements: 2½ inches long x 1¾ inches wide. Photo by Sunny Sung.

American mastodon tooth; genus: *Mammut;* epoch: Pliocene; location: Peace River; county: Hardee; measurements 4½ inches long x 4 inches wide x 5 inches deep. Photo by author.

Mastodon ankle bone (astragalus); genus: *Mammut;* epoch: Pliocene; location: Peace River; county: Hardee; measurements: 6 inches long x 4½ inches wide x 4 inches thick. Photo by Sunny Sung.

American mastodon toe bones; genus: *Mammut;* epoch: Pliocene; location: Peace River; county: Hardee; measurements: larger bone is 5 inches long x 2½ inches thick. Photo by Sunny Sung.

Peccary
Family: Tayassuidae

Peccary upper tusk; species: undetermined; epoch: Pleistocene; location: Joshua Creek; county: DeSoto; measurements: 4 inches long x ¾ inch wide x ½ inch thick. Photo by Sunny Sung.

Sharks
Family: Odontaspidae

Sand tiger shark tooth (top) and extinct sand shark tooth (bottom); species: *Odontaspis taurus* (top), *Odontaspis cuspidata* (bottom); epoch: Oligocene to Miocene (bottom), Miocene to recent (top); location: Peace River (top), Venice Beach (bottom); county: Polk (top) and Sarasota (bottom); measurements: about 1 inch for both. Photo by Sunny Sung.

Family: Isuridae

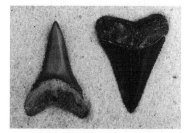

Great white shark teeth (wider tooth is an upper); species: *Carcharodon carcharias;* epoch: Pleistocene to recent; location: Caloosahatchee River; county: Hendry; measurements: large one is 1¼ inches long. Photo by Sunny Sung.

Extinct giant white tooth; species: *Carcharodon megalodon;* epoch: Miocene; location: Myakkahatchee Creek; county: Sarasota; measurements: 5½ inches x 4 inches. Back side of tooth. Photo by Sunny Sung.

Extinct giant white tooth (looks like back side of tooth but is actually the front, or what you would see as the shark opens its mouth); species: *Carcharodon megalodon;* epoch: Miocene; location: Venice Beach; county: Sarasota; measurements: 5 inches long. Photo by Sunny Sung.

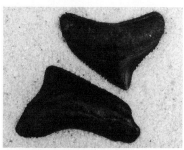

Extinct giant white rear teeth; species: *Carcharodon megalodon;* epoch: Miocene; location: Peace River; county: Hardee; measurements: 1 inch x ¾ inch. Photo by Sunny Sung.

Mako teeth (larger tooth is an upper); species: *Isurus hastalis;* epoch: Miocene to Pliocene; location: Myakkahatchee River (larger), Caloosahatchee River (smaller); county: Sarasota (larger), Lee (smaller); measurements: larger one is 1¾ inches long x 1¼ inches wide. Photo by Sunny Sung.

Family: Charcharhinidae (requiem sharks)

Tiger shark teeth; species: *Galeocerdo cuvieri;* epoch: Miocene to recent; location: Peace River; county: Hardee; measurements: 1 inch x 1 inch. Photo by author.

Extinct snaggletooth shark teeth (larger tooth is an upper); species: *Hemipristis serra;* epoch: Miocene to Pliocene; location: Caloosahatchee River; county: Hendry; measurements: larger one is 1½ inches x 1 inch. Photo by Sunny Sung.

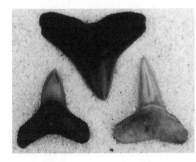

Left to right: bull, dusky (above other two), lemon sharks. Photo by Sunny Sung. Bull shark tooth; species: *Carcharhinus leucas;* epoch: Miocene to recent; location: Peace River; county: Hardee; measurements: ½ inch wide across root x ½ inch deep. Dusky shark tooth; species: *Carcharhinus obscurus;* epoch: Miocene to recent; location: Peace River; county: Hardee; measurements: ⅝ inch across root x ½ inch deep. Lemon shark tooth; species: *Negaprion brevirostris;* epoch: Oligocene to recent; location: Joshua Creek; county: DeSoto; measurements: ⅝ inch wide across root x 7/16 inch deep.

Dusky shark tooth stuck in limestone rock. Photo by Sunny Sung.

Cow shark teeth (large tooth is an upper, small teeth are lowers); species: undetermined; epoch: undetermined; location: Caloosahatchee River (large), Peace River (small); county: Lee (large) and Hardee (small); measurements: large one is 1 inch long x ⅛ inch wide x ½ inch deep. Photo by Sunny Sung.

Sloths
Family: Edentates

Giant ground sloth claws; genus: *Eremotherium;* epoch: Pleistocene; location: shallow creek; county: DeSoto; measurements: 15½ inches long (left) and 16½ inches long. Photo by Sunny Sung.

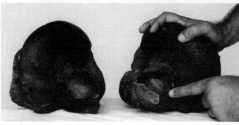

Giant ground sloth ankle bone (astragalus); genus: *Eremotherium;* epoch: Pleistocene; location: Prairie Creek; county: DeSoto; measurements: 8 inches wide x 8 inches tall. Photo by Sunny Sung.

Family: Megalonychidae

Ground sloth tooth; species: *Glossotherium harlani;* epoch: Pleistocene; location: Prairie Creek; county: DeSoto; measurements: 3 inches tall x 2¾ inches wide. Photo by Sunny Sung.

Ground sloth tooth (lower); species: *Glossotherium harlani;* epoch: Pleistocene; location: Charlie Apopka Creek; county: Hardee; measurements: 2½ inches long x 1 inch wide. Photo by Sunny Sung.

Family: Mylodontidae

Ground sloth tooth; genus: *Glossotherium;* epoch: Pleistocene; location: Prairie Creek; county: DeSoto; measurements: 2¾ inches long x 1 inch wide. Photo by Sunny Sung.

Ground sloth tooth; species: *Glossotherium harlani;* epoch: Pleistocene; location: Joshua Creek; county: DeSoto; measurements: 2½ inch x ¾ inch. Photo by Sunny Sung.

Ground sloth tooth; genus: *Glossotherium;* epoch: Pleistocene; location: Prairie Creek; county: DeSoto; measurements: 2⅝ inches long x 1 inch wide. Photo by Sunny Sung.

Ground sloth foot bone; genus: *Glossotherium;* epoch: Pleistocene; location: DeSoto County Creek; measurements: 2 inches x 1¾ inches x ¾ inch thick. Photo by Sunny Sung.

Ground sloth ankle bone (astragalus); genus: *Glossotherium;* epoch: Pleistocene; location: Prairie Creek; county: DeSoto; measurements: 3 inches wide x 2½ inches tall. Photo by Sunny Sung.

Tapir
Family: Tapiridae

Tapir molar; genus: *Tapirus;* epoch: Pleistocene; location: Peace River; county: Hardee; measurements: 1 inch across crown x 1¼ inches deep. Photo by Sunny Sung.

Tapir last molar; genus: *Tapirus;* epoch: Pleistocene; location: shallow creek; county: DeSoto; measurements: crown is 1 inch long x 1 inch tall x ½ inch wide. Photo by author.

Tapir molars; genus: *Tapirus;* epoch: Pleistocene; location: Peace River; county: Hardee; measurements: tooth with roots is 1 inch across crown x 1¼ inches deep. Photo by Sunny Sung.

Tapir mandible with teeth; genus: *Tapirus;* epoch: Pleistocene; location: Peace River; county: Hardee; measurements: 5½ inches long x 1¼ inches wide x 3½ inches high. Photo by author.

Tortoise
Family: Testudinidae

Giant land tortoise hoof core; genus: *Geochelone;* epoch: Pleistocene; location: Prairie Creek; county: DeSoto; measurements: 2 inches long x ⅝ inch wide. Photo by Sunny Sung.

Giant land tortoise shell fragment; genus: *Geochelone;* epoch: Pleistocene; location: Joshua Creek; county: DeSoto; measurements: 9 inches across x 1½ inches thick. Photo by Sunny Sung.

Giant land tortoise shell fragment; genus: *Geochelone;* epoch: Pleistocene; location: Joshua Creek; county: DeSoto; measurements: 7 inches across x 1 inch thick. Photo by Sunny Sung.

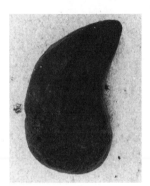

Giant land tortoise fighting/mating spur; genus: *Geochelone;* epoch: Pleistocene; location: Myakka River; county: Sarasota; measurements: 1¼ inches long x ⅝ inch thick. Photo by Sunny Sung.

Giant land tortoise foot pads; genus: *Geochelone;* epoch: Pleistocene; location: Hawthorne Creek; county: DeSoto; measurements: 2 inches across x ½ inch thick. Photo by author.

Giant land tortoise—end of femur; genus: *Geochelone;* epoch: Pleistocene; location: Joshua Creek; county: DeSoto; measurements: 3 inches thick. Photo by Sunny Sung.

Pond Turtle
Family: Emydidae

Pond turtle shell fragments; genus: *Pseudemys;* epoch: Pleistocene; location: Caloosahatchee River; county: Hendry; measurements: largest one is 2 inches x 1¾ inches. Photo by Sunny Sung.

Pond turtle nuccal scute; genus: *Pseudemys;* epoch: Pleistocene; location: Caloosahatchee River; county: Hendry; measurements: 2½ inches x 2¼ inches. Photo by Sunny Sung.

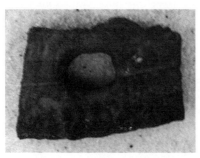

Pond turtle shell fragment with hole from gator bite; genus: *Pseudemys;* epoch: Pleistocene; location: Prairie Creek; county: DeSoto; measurements: 2½ inches long x 1 inch wide x ¼ inch thick. Photo by Sunny Sung.

Box turtle
Family: Emydidae

Box turtle trap door (undershell); species: *Terrapene carolina;* epoch: Pleistocene; location: Peace River; county: Hardee; measurements: 4½ inches long x 3½ inches wide. Photo by Sunny Sung.

Whale

Order: Cetacea
Suborder: Odontoceti (toothed whales and dolphins)

Sperm whale tooth; genus: unknown; epoch: Pliocene; location: shallow creek; county: DeSoto; measurements: 5 inches long x 1¼ inches wide. Photo by author.

Suborder: Mysticeti (baleen or whalebone whales)

Whale neck vertebra; genus: unknown; epoch: Pliocene; location: Caloosahatchee River; county: Hendry; measurements: 7 inches long x 5 inches wide x 2¼ inches thick. Photo by Sunny Sung.

Whale vertebra; genus: unknown; epoch: Pliocene; location: Venice Beach; county: Sarasota; measurements: 5 inches tall x 4 inches thick. Photo by Sunny Sung.

Whale bulla (ear bones); genus: *Baleonoptera* (left) and *Eubalaena* (right); epoch: Pliocene (left), Miocene (right); location: Orange River (left), Venice Beach (right); county: Lee (left), Sarasota (right); measurements 2½ inches long x 1¾ inches wide (left), 4 inches long x 3 inches wide (right). Photo by Sunny Sung.

Artifacts (Please refer to chapter 21 on legalities)

Seminoles poling a dugout canoe through Big Cypress Preserve in the Everglades. Photo by author.

Native Americans often used deer antler bases for knife blade handles. This knife belongs to a modern Seminole on Big Cypress Preserve in the Everglades. Photo by author.

Potsherd. A broken piece of pottery (DeSoto County creek) will often resemble a piece of turtle shell, except that its finish is coarse like sandpaper and it breaks easily; measurements: 4 inches across top x 3 inches wide x ¼ inch thick. Photo by author.

Deer's ear carved from pottery, 2¼ inches long. Unearthed by bulldozer during development of site. Choko-loskee Island, Collier County. Photo by author.

Citrus point, 4 inches long, DeSoto County creek. Photo by author.

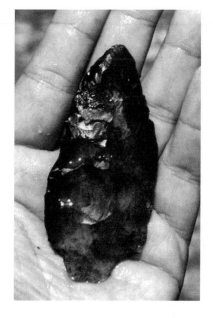

Thonotosassa point, 3¾ inches long. Used as a thrusting spear, dagger, or knife. Peace River, Hardee County. Photo by author.

Tanged point, 3 inches long, DeSoto County creek. Photo by author.

Possible Marion point, 3 inches long, DeSoto County creek. Photo by author.

Bird point, ½ inch long, DeSoto County creek. Photo by author.

Flint scraper, 1½ inches long, Santa Fe River, Gilchrist County. Photo by author.

Deer antler, 3½ inches long, worked into a spike, possibly as building material, DeSoto County creek. Photo by author.

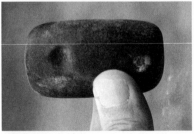

Possible hammer, 2½ inches long, made of dugong rib, Peace River, Hardee County. Photo by author.

Bone pins made mostly from deer bones, ranging from 2 inches to 3½ inches long. Used as hairpins or for sewing. From various Florida creeks and rivers. Photo by author.

Flint chopping tool, 7 inches long x 3½ inches wide x 2 inches thick, Gilchrist County. Photo by Sunny Sung.

Right: Same flint chopping tool, different angle. Photo by Sunny Sung.

Whelk shell tool, 3¼ inches long x 3 inches thick. Hole was drilled and a stick run through it for use as a tool or weapon. Note wear at narrow end of shell. Unearthed by bulldozer during development of site. Chokoloskee Island, Collier County. Photo by Sunny Sung.

Small shells, possibly used as earrings or other body ornaments, 1¾ inches long x 1¼ inches wide, unearthed by bulldozer during development of site. Chokoloskee Island, Collier County. Photo by author.

Ceremonial ax head, 4 inches long x 2½ inches wide x ¾ inch thick, Lee County. Probably a traded item because type of stone is not native to Florida. Photo by author.

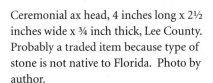

17

How to Keep Them Around for Another Million Years

Bone Preservatives

An entire ice age has come and gone since the creature died. Its limb bone lay buried all this time in a protective coating of sand—until today. That's when the steady flow of the river this year finally cut through the sediments of time and exposed the bone. You happened along and picked it up, knowing right away it was a prize. Now, how do you preserve it for another million years?

Some bones will never need a helping hand. They're solid enough to sit on a shelf just as they are, and should suffer no damage from continually being picked up and admired, and occasionally dropped. Others may need your expertise as a bone surgeon to have them reconstructed and better preserved.

If a bone is resting on a creek bed and appears to be free of any restricting material holding it in place, there is a good chance it will be sturdy enough for you to pick it up without wrapping anything around it. But if it's buried

This giant land tortoise shell had to be reassembled. From the collection of the Florida Museum of Natural History, Gainesville. Photo by Robin Brown.

in soft limestone or other material, it may begin to fall apart as soon as you try to dislodge it. For times like this, carry along aluminum foil on your fossil expeditions, or at least a plastic sandwich bag to hold the pieces together until you get home.

Don't scrape all the material from around the bone. Use it to your advantage by allowing it to help hold the bone together. If the material around the bone is soft enough, dig a small trench under the bone (in water or dry land). Then wrap aluminum foil around the fossil. If it appears really fragile, see if you can find a piece of wood to use as a splint to keep it from breaking.

If you've come across something fragile that is too big to wrap in aluminum foil, you may have to use a plaster jacket. Although you won't be able to apply it under water, you will need water for the task. You'll also need a bucket, toilet paper (nonscented) or paper towels, burlap, trowel, and a permanent marking pen. (For underwater jackets, 3M has a product called Scotchcast that sets up in 15 or 20 minutes. It's expensive and is available from surgical supply stores.)

Clear off enough clay or limestone to get an idea how long and large the fossil is. Pack it back on afterward. Dig a trench underneath, allowing for plenty of matrix between the bone and your trowel. You should end up with the bone sitting on a natural pedestal.

Dampen enough paper towels or toilet paper to cover the exposed bone, so it won't stick to the plaster. Cut the burlap into strips as wide (four inches is average) and long as you need them for the size of bone you're covering. Dip the burlap in plaster of paris mixed with water to the consistency of cream. Squeeze the burlap gently and apply it in a cross-thread pattern over the bone until it's at least a quarter inch thick.

If it's a particularly heavy bone that you may have trouble picking up, place sticks or pieces of flat wood under the bone, and then apply the plaster-coated burlap over it. Leave enough of the wood on both ends so that you have something to hold.

Plaster of paris takes about 45 minutes to dry. When it's dry, use your marking pen to log the type of fossil, date, and site, then sketch the fossil's outline on the jacket. That way you'll know which side is up or down when it's time to unwrap it. Also note the formation or type of sediments in which it was buried.

Once it's dry, you can gently remove your find from its pedestal, turn it over, and wrap the bottom if needed.

Important: If you find a whole fossilized skeleton laid out as if every bone is in place, don't rush in and start digging it up. It may be of significance to scientists. Stop everything, find a phone, and call the Florida Museum of Natural History in Gainesville, (352) 392-1721. Describe what you have found, and a staff member will tell you if it is something that interests the museum or if it's a common find. The museum will then do one of three things: (1) it will send out a staff member if it is able and the rarity of your find warrants it; (2) it will contact knowledgeable amateurs who live in most parts of the state and are glad to serve as "minutemen"; or (3) it will at least give you some direction on how to recover your find.

Let's say you come across a partial skeleton that is *not* complete—or articulated—and the bones appear fractured and broken up. Just because this site may not be important to paleontologists does not mean it has no archaeological significance. Native Americans often used the bones and teeth of the animals they butchered for tools and weapons.

Examine your fossils carefully. Remember, too, that a lot of marks on them may have been caused by whatever predator killed them, or scavengers cleaning the carcass afterward, or other hoofed animals walking and running over the scattered bones.

If they are marine mammal bones you have uncovered, do the marks look like they could have been made by a shark? Are there several rows of scratches about the same distance apart as if they were bite marks? If it's a land animal, how about an alligator, cat, dog, or wolf? What about vultures scraping the bone as they removed the meat?

Marks made by humans are not always easy to recognize, but there are signs you can look for. If it's a bone, does it appear to have been sharpened and sanded evenly all the way around the base? Do the markings appear as if something was chewing or gnawing, or do they seem more purposeful? Does the bone look as if it would be useful as a tool? Are there holes drilled through it? (But note it's not uncommon to find bones with holes in them drilled by marine organisms at the time the animal died.)

Overall, just use common sense. You don't want to be calling the Florida Bureau of Archaeological Research in Tallahassee, (850) 487-2299, for every little scratch, but the bureau does want to encourage your inquiries. Also see chapter 21, "Staying Out of Trouble."

Nonfragile fossils can be cleaned with a paintbrush or toothbrush under running water. If a sturdy bone needs repairing, dry it first. Use Butvar (a museum glue) or acrylic B-72. Florida Museum of Natural History preparator Russ McCarty explains this process on the museum's web site (http://www.flmnh.ufl.edu/natsci/vertpaleo/resources/prep.htm).

White glue is acidic and is not good for fossils. If your fossil turns out to be important to scientists, they may want to take Scanning Electron Microscope images of marks or features on it. The images in turn may be used to determine how an animal used its tusks or teeth, whether it had a disease, or had been wounded or killed and eaten by a carnivore, or butchered by a person using a flint knife. White glue eliminates the possibility of SEM analysis.

For smaller bone specimens, you might consider an acetone bath method as an alternative. Be aware that acetone has noxious fumes and is very flammable. Again, refer to the Florida Museum of Natural History's web site.

After specimens are repaired, allow several weeks for the fossil to dry before applying a hardener. Many museums use a hardener that is a mixture of one ounce of Butvar-76 and five ounces of acetone. Check with the Florida Museum of Natural History or the Florida Paleontological Society to purchase the Butvar, (352) 392-1721. Acetone is available at most hardware stores. In the absence of Butvar, some fossilers use hardeners that are about 25 percent glue and 75 percent water.

To open your plaster jacket for preservation, saw around the top with a small hand saw. Make sure everything is dry before continuing. Clean your specimen with a dental pick and brush, then apply bone hardener gradually, repairing parts as needed.

To label your fossil afterward, use gesso primer for canvas to paint a white strip. Once it is dry, use a waterproof ink such as India Ink to mark the specimen.

Assign it a code such as OR29 (Orange River, 29th specimen). Then make an accompanying file card, including such information as type of animal, part of anatomy, location found, formation or sediment, conditions (high water, low, excavated pit, creek, etc.), name of person who found it, and date. Arrange your file cards in a way that is easy for you to reference later. As you build your collection, you might want to transfer your files to computer for easier cross-indexing.

18

Hunters' Hazards from
Boats to Barbed Wire

The 60-foot giant white shark has been extinct for five million years. To get one of its prized six-inch teeth, all you have to do is make your way to an area in which the huge monster once existed and start looking, right? Wrong.

There is a little-known addendum to Murphy's Law that you, the fossil hunter, must learn: There's always something guarding the treasure. It's important for you to remember that. For every hunt upon which you embark, something will be standing between you and the choicest fossils.

You have not been truly indoctrinated into the world of old bones until you have encountered at least three "treasure guardians" at one time. Some are just a wee bit annoying. Others may be extremely hazardous to your health. You must be the final judge as to whether the treasure is worth trying to face or bypass whatever (or whoever) is guarding it.

For example, I loaded all my fossil gear into my canoe one sunny afternoon and headed up the Peace River in DeSoto County. As I approached the spot in which several mastodons, sloths, and giant white sharks surely were buried, it began to rain. It rained so hard, I thought for sure my canoe would fill up with water and sink. So I paddled under the branches of a large oak tree growing out of the bank.

Unfortunately, every mosquito within a 20-mile radius got the same idea. Before I could swat the first 10,000 or so, lightning began to dance all around me and an alligator surfaced where I had planned to enter the water. I decided to take a rain check on the fossiling and rowed in Olympic fashion back to the safety of my car.

Here is a partial list of treasure guardians you, too, may look forward to enjoying:

Fire Ants. It seems to me that there are more fire ants in a square mile than there are people in the entire state of Florida. Their favorite time to bite is when you are hopping around on one foot, trying to put on your wet suit. The secret to avoiding a confrontation with these nasty little buggers is to (1) stay in your car and take a nap while the others go fossiling, (2) get out of your car and pretend you're the retired star of *River Dance* while donning your suit, and (3) stay home and wait around to see if any animals die and become fossilized in your backyard.

If you think you might be safer in the water, think again. There have been times when I have found a fantastic fossil site in about two feet of water. While I was snorkeling, with only my neck and head out of the water, a herd of several hundred fire ants had the audacity to form a floating island upstream. Then they took advantage of the current to deliver themselves downstream until they got to my unsuspecting neck. Scaling it like a red wiggly necklace, they wanted to see which one could inflict the largest welt. I'd rather swim with piranhas.

Barbed Wire Fences. Some famous person once said that great fences make great neighbors. But another famous person said "phooey" to that. Personally, I've never known anyone who was fond of a neighbor who put up a barbed wire fence. Yes, they keep cattle in. But they also keep serious-minded fossil hunters out.

Most fences you're going to encounter will be strung strategically across whatever creek or river you're curious about exploring. Rather than cut the wire or climb over or under, I recommend that you first try to find out who owns the fence and see if you can get permission to use the gate. It may save you from spending your weekend behind bars or attempting to drive home with a heinie full of buckshot.

"No Trespassing" Signs. You'll usually encounter them any place where someone other than you owns the property. Most people who put them up don't have anything better to do than arrest you for pretending the signs don't exist. Your best bet, just as with barbed wire fences, is to get permission to go around them. If that doesn't work, heed them.

Just because a private property owner may be legally polluting the environment, clearing the land of its natural vegetation and critters to build a new golf course or yet another condominium complex, you don't have a right to go in under his or her nose and look for some new creature that might actually benefit science.

Bovine Beasts. If you live in Florida, you're bound to run into such an animal sooner or later. I recently took what I thought was a shortcut across a field while returning from a fossil outing. A large herd of cows was grazing contentedly between me and the most direct route home. I was considering an alternate field that might prove safer, until I saw a lone bull eyeballing me as if he was experienced at this type of fossil warfare.

Which field would you cross? I choose the one more traveled and that made all the difference in the world. Cows are usually very timid. But bulls possess what is commonly referred to as "testicular fortitude." When I traipsed through the cow pasture, dodging all those foul-smelling land mines, they scattered as if I was the neighborhood butcher.

Alligators. *Respect* is the key word here. Show plenty of respect, especially if you happen to encounter an alligator while you're in the water. Particularly if that alligator is large enough to swallow the biggest lie you've ever told. For the most part, a gator would much rather dine on small, tasty fish and softshell turtles than your preservative-filled body. But if it has been fed by humans, it may have trouble telling the difference between a hand and a handout. Alligators can be even more dangerous when breeding or caring for their babies. Give them as much room as you would an approaching aircraft carrier or a religious zealot.

Rain. During the dry season, many Florida creeks and rivers contain shallows measuring one foot to three feet in depth. But during the rainy season, those same bodies of water may swell to the size of the Mississippi and the depth of the Pacific Ocean. With the increased depth, you'll find the water more murky and faster moving. If you're a diver, you may have to don scuba gear and use a dive light. Or you may be better off hiring someone else to do your diving for you.

Lightning. Florida has more lightning than almost any other state in the nation. Here, it might strike not only twice in the same spot but also where the best fossils are buried. Since storm clouds form more often in the afternoon than the morning during the rainy season, conquer this treasure guardian by doing your searching early in the day or at night.

Mosquitoes. They're the original back stabbers. They'll buzz around in front of your face, pretending to be harmless gnats, but as soon as you bend over to check out a fossil, they'll put it to you from behind. Only the females bite, which is probably just nature's way of getting even with men for all the times they leave the toilet seat up. These kamikazes of the insect world tend to congregate on riverbanks, again, where the best fossils are located. Combat them by applying Deep-Woods OFF, or avoid fossiling in the early morning or evening when they're the most passionate.

Noseums (pronounced no-see-ums). A better name for these nearly invisible winged beasts should be surfelums (pronounced sure-feel-ums). They hurt more than mosquito bites, and it really is difficult to see them because they're so small. If Avon-Skin-So-Soft won't do the trick, hunt only when it snows.

Sand Spurs. These prickly weeds like to hide where only the barest feet, ankles, and legs dare to tread. Once they poke you, their barbs break off under your skin, and unless you own a miniature crowbar or your fossil partner is a medical doctor, you can't pry them out for weeks.

Large Boats with Large Wakes. Okay, so you want to do your part to preserve nature and disturb as little of it as possible when you're fossiling. Well, don't expect the rest of the world to pat you on the back and watch out for you on the open water. My first two years fossiling, I paddled a canoe up and down the Caloosahatchee River, feeling smitten that I hadn't chewed up any manatees or disrupted surface fish with a powerful outboard motor that might also scare away wading birds. My reward? Rather than slow down when approaching me on the river, many operators of large vessels maintain full speed and actually wave smilingly as they launch six-foot waves at my canoe. Lately, I've been thinking of manufacturing my own specialized line of Uzzis.

Sharks. They're no problem as long as you stay out of the water. Actually, one of the few places you'll have to worry about them is diving at places like Venice Beach. But to my knowledge, no shark has ever attacked a diver or swimmer there. It's more likely that you'll cut yourself on a shell or have your feet trampled on by 300 other vacationers wanting to occupy the same square foot of beach you're standing on. Still, since I saw the movie *Jaws,* it's been difficult focusing 100 percent on fossiling once I leave the dry world. I just know that every shadow, every strange sound, may turn out to be a toothy man-eater from the Pleistocene epoch, on the prowl for human sushi.

Snakes. For some reason, I used to think snakes swim only on the surface, so you can see them in time to get out of their way. Not true. I recently watched a Florida cottonmouth swim gracefully along the bottom of a creek where I had been standing only moments before. These venomous reptiles are at home in the water, on dry ground, or even in your canoe. The only thing they fear is a bigger cottonmouth. To avoid them and their potentially fatal bite, it's best not to get in the water when they're mating (May and June), raising their young (July and August), or resting after the ordeal (September through April). Any other time is fine.

Heat. While all the other treasure guardians will affect you immediately, the greatest danger from the sun probably won't do its damage for a number of years. Spend too much time in the sun, and not only will your skin gradually burn to the consistency of a raisin, but you're also likely to develop a skin condition that may limit the number of golden years you might otherwise enjoy. Applying lots of sunblock helps, but you're far better off covering your body with clothing and keeping a wet towel around your neck on hot days.

When it come to other guardians of the treasure, such as poison ivy and fellow fossilers who beat you to the best spots, you can rest assured that they will present themselves to you when you least expect it. Whatever you do, don't make a big deal of it, because Murphy's Law, section 8, paragraph 2C, states explicitly, "There's always something guarding the treasure."

19

And Then Came Man . . .

The Role of Early Humans in Pleistocene Extinctions

The unspoiled Aucilla River begins its 69-mile flow to the Gulf of Mexico in southern Georgia. A favorite waterway for canoeists in Florida's Big Bend, the river forms the boundary between Jefferson and Taylor counties. But long before the river was considered a recreational getaway by modern man, it had an extensive history of human habitation.

Since 1983, a small, ever-changing group of die-hard professional and amateur scientists have worked for a couple of months each year on what has become known as the Aucilla River Prehistory Project. Cosponsored by the Florida Museum of Natural History, the Department of State's Division of Historic Resources, and the National Geographic Society, the project is attempting to answer some of the following questions:

- When did the first humans arrive in Florida? How did they get here?

- What was their role in the demise of many prehistoric animals now extinct in our state?
- How did Paleo people survive in Florida?
- What effect did climatic and environmental changes of 10,000 to 15,000 years ago have on the vegetation and wildlife, as well as the lifestyle of these early settlers?

Here is what the project has turned up so far:

- Seventy-five archaeological sites exist in or near the Aucilla River. More than 3,000 bone, stone, and wood artifacts have been recovered from underwater sites near Nuttall Rise alone.
- An 11,000-year-old *Bison antiquus* skull found in the Wacissa River, near where it meets up with the Aucilla, provided the inspiration for the project. Embedded in the skull was a broken spear tip.

Aucilla River. Photo by Robin Brown.

- A 12,200-year-old, seven-and-a-half-foot mastodon tusk was found with butcher marks, suggesting it was cut out of the animal's skull with stone knives, possibly for ivory to make tools. The site is the earliest known "butcher" shop in North America. Because the tusks are 700 years older than any site so far uncovered in the western United States, scientists wonder if humans may have migrated to lower latitudes through an eastern passage rather than the far West as traditionally thought.

- One of the world's richest collections of prehistoric-worked ivory was donated to the Florida Museum of Natural History by Dr. Richard Ohmes and his son, Donald. Found in the Aucilla and Wacissa, the finds include a complete ivory foreshaft pin bearing a decorative design on each side. It is the oldest artwork in North America.

- While the tossed and tumbled sediments along most of Florida's river and creek beds make it tough to accurately date bones and other material, the Aucilla holds a well-layered and preserved record of time.

- Well-preserved mastodon dung has been collected, shedding light on this unique proboscidian's diet, as well as providing additional proof of the site's outstanding preservative qualities. DNA and steroids have been extracted from this material.

- From sediment samples which sometimes contain seeds, leaves, and twigs, paleobotanists have already been able to decipher weather patterns, determine when a plant or tree began growing in this part of the world, and when it altered its form or died out altogether.

The Aucilla's numerous sites continue to offer scientists a chance to search for in-place human artifacts to more accurately date the approximate century—even the season—they were last used. We know that humans had at least a minor role in forcing some of the larger prehistoric mammals into extinction because they were all creatures we hunted. But it's still too early to determine if our role was a major one, or if environmental changes may have brought on the mass extinctions.

Perhaps we will soon find out exactly what wiped out such unusual animals as saber-toothed cats and giant ground sloths. Or we will discover precisely when humans first entered peninsular Florida and from which direction. When all is said and done, maybe we'll discover that the earliest residents were snowbirds from Ohio, and that their first observation was how much better things were in the North.

20

Florida's Lost City of Atlantis

Just as that curmudgeon of a philosopher Henry David Thoreau journeyed inside his mind for two years at Walden Pond, my two weeks at the Aucilla River were a mental sojourn. But unlike Thoreau, who returned to civilization with many more answers than questions about why humans behave as they do, I came away even more curious about Paleo people and their relationship to their environment than when I first arrived at this remarkable river.

It's one thing to read about such ancient sites as the Aucilla holds, but to actually participate in underwater excavations as a volunteer and explore the remnants of this long-ago world firsthand is likened to diving in search of the lost city of Atlantis.

In spite of having permission to be there, I couldn't help but feel like a trespasser as I drove onto the site. Who was I to come traipsing into the past, taking part in disturbing over 12,000 years of a buried way of life? I quickly assured myself that my intentions as an amateur, as well as those of the professionals I would soon be working with, were honorable. We were coming here to better understand a way of life, one which is tied to us as intrinsically as the immediate generation before us. Because, like it or not, we are all interconnected by time and space, no matter where we were born.

I wish I had some kind of crystal ball that would allow me to gaze into the past. The Aucilla, like many other Florida rivers, didn't exist 12,000 years ago. Instead, freshwater springs and water-filled sinkholes dotted the region. Animals and humans frequented these spots not only to drink but to hunt one another. At night, the humans would squat next to a Paleo campfire and sample some of the local chef's mammoth chops, deer burgers, side-of-sloth or sabercat stew. After dinner, there would be family fireside chats in whatever strange dialects these people spoke.

How frightened were they about what lay beyond their campsite and the protection they received in armed numbers? Did they view themselves as the dominant life form for their world or as an equal, fighting for survival like all the other animals? Did they sit and stare up at the stars on a clear night with the same awe as we do today?

What were the roles of the women and men, as well as the children? What did they do when they were just goofing off? What games did they play? Did they have weather forecasters, and were they as off base as those we watch on television today?

And what about their reverence for life? When they killed a mastodon, did it disturb them to see it die, even though they were killing for food and other necessities? Or did they brag about the size of its tusks the same way hunters today gleefully display the size of a deer's rack? Did they observe the social interaction between mastodons the way we do elephants? Elephants have been seen standing guard over their dead and "burying" them by piling leaves and twigs on their bodies. If the two proboscidians' behavior patterns were similar, then mammoths and mastodons, like elephants, may have gone through a mourning process when one of their group died.

I would also look into the future with that crystal ball and perhaps see my own culture studied by future scientists. I personally can think of no greater contribution to humankind after I die than to have my bones, my work space, my living quarters, the tools I handle every day—whether they be a computer, a toothbrush, or electric razor—studied under some distant generation's microscope. For better or worse, think what could be learned from our culture!

My two weeks at the site were not what I had expected, although the work was challenging. In two-person teams, each of us had to dive down to an oak tree resting on the site and, with bow saw in hand, cut off the large overhanging branches that might later snag our dive gear as we worked. Visibility was so poor you couldn't see your hand in front of your face. So one person sawed while the other held a powerful dive light driven by a generator on dry land. Breathing was accomplished not by tanks but by a Brownie Third Lung, which is a compressor that feeds fresh air to divers. The balance of the two weeks consisted of two-person, two-hour shifts excavating and collecting sediment samples every 20 centimeters to the bottom.

During excavations—conducted with a hand trowel—a bone pin, bifacial chopper tool, flint flake, and unidentifiable point (stem was missing) turned up. However, since the items were not found wedged in place within sediments, but rather lying on the surface or sucked up in the debris-clearing dredge, it will be difficult to give them a precise date.

And then there was the mastodon grave in 30 feet of water. The sediments at that depth are 31,000 years old. That probably means the animal died then. But careful analysis of its context will be made to determine whether it may have been washed down from a higher and more recent elevation.

The amateur and professional crew itself was a hodgepodge of women and men from all over the United States. They were from such states as Arizona, Illinois, Virginia, Georgia, and Florida. Among their occupations were welder, veterinarian, dentist, soldier, dive instructor, and undergraduate archaeology student. Their ages ranged from 20 to 71.

Once all the data for this project are assimilated and articles are published, we should all know considerably more about Florida's first residents—and perhaps even ourselves. Who we are, and how we became who we are, have a lot to do with who our ancestors were. The better we understand the mechanics of our past, the better equipped we will be to cope with the present and future.

21

Staying Out of Trouble

A Layperson's Lesson in Legalities

While this book is chiefly about hunting for the bones and teeth of ancient animals, one can't help but occasionally stumble across Native American artifacts in that pursuit. And because the sciences of paleontology and archaeology overlap in so many areas, laws governing both disciplines are included in this chapter.

No one can deny that amateurs are responsible for a great many significant discoveries in both sciences, but it is also true that amateurs have been responsible—intentionally and unintentionally—for the destruction of many historic (archaeology) and prehistoric (usually paleontology, sometimes archaeology or a combination of the two if human artifacts are found in association with ancient animals) sites.

The unintentional destruction that we amateurs cause can add up to major headaches and heartaches for the professional community. For instance, while fossil hunting with scuba gear, an amateur comes across mastodon bones partially buried on the bottom of a river. He's interested only in the three teeth and a partial tusk he finds mixed with the bones, so

A 3-inch-long Simpson point from the late Paleo period (10,000 to 11,000 years B.P.). Florida law requires that all artifacts be reported to the Bureau of Archaeological Research in Tallahassee. Peace River, Hardee County. Photo by author.

he leaves the rest behind. Later, a professional team of divers from a local university searches the same area for connections between early humans and the extinction of such animals as the mastodon at the close of the last ice age. They find the bones, but the teeth, which may have helped provide clues as to the mastodon's precise diet, are missing. The tusk, which had butcher marks on it indicating it may have been killed by ancient man, is also gone. It might have told scientists if and approximately when the mastodon was killed by humans.

With a small trowel, the amateur fossiler had also scraped away at the river bottom in search of fossils below the top layer of sediments. The harm here is that in certain Florida rivers, these sediments were laid down and preserved in the exact order in which time progressed. When the bottom is disturbed by an amateur fossiler, the context of the different layers is compromised.

In another scenario, an amateur discovers the skull of a rare prehistoric animal. He offers the skull to his state museum knowing it doesn't have such a specimen, but the museum cannot afford to buy it for the asking price. So the finder instead sells it to an out-of-state or out-of-country buyer, who resells it again at a higher price. As a result, the skull is not available for local or visiting paleontologists to study, or to compare as other similar finds are collected. Also, if it is a new genus or species, it will not be identified or named without scientific examination and comparison. So everyone loses.

In archaeology, we all know someone—perhaps ourselves—who has visited a historic site and picked up or broken off a small souvenir to take home and set on the mantel. Maybe it was a piece of pottery on the ground or a chip of stone from an already decaying historic structure. No one will notice one little piece missing, we reason, until we step back and see that thousands of people removing "one little piece" have significantly altered a site for archaeologists to study and future generations to appreciate.

Amateur archaeology and paleontology do not have to be destructive pastimes. There are responsible ways to search out the past and share that information with science—most of them involving plain old common sense.

For instance, if you carry a shovel into a shallow creek or river while looking for shark teeth, limit your digging to gravelly areas that look as if the bottom has been all stirred up by the current or a previous ice-age ocean. And if you come across something that appears to be significant, stop working immediately and call a professional.

If you decide to investigate a riverbank for fossils, use what I call "low-impact" digging. Use a small garden shovel or, better still, a dive knife or screwdriver. Poke around gingerly for isolated fossils, and, again, if you happen to stumble onto an entire something-or-other, stop and make that phone call.

And here's where it gets sticky when you are holding a shovel or other digging device. In most cases it is legal for you to dig with a hand shovel for fossils (not artifacts) in a creek or riverbed bordered by private property. But you may still need to get permission from the landowner, especially if there is some question as to his or her waterway rights.

In most situations you are also allowed to dig for fossils in a streambed owned by the state, providing it doesn't border a state or federal park or preserve, or there are no other restrictions regarding that specific site. You must also have obtained a fossil permit from the state. (The application process is discussed later in this chapter.)

But the state antiquity law CH 267 FS does not allow you to search (digging or otherwise) for artifacts on state-owned or controlled uplands or submerged lands without written authorization (permit or contract).

The only exception is for the surface collection (again, not digging)—while snorkeling, diving, or walking and stooping—of isolated artifacts from Florida rivers, which does not require a permit but does require that you report your finds for them to be legal.

Law enforcement officers have been warning, ticketing, and, in some instances, arresting artifact collectors found using hand tools such as forks and shovels in Florida rivers. You should also be aware that underwater archaeological sites such as shipwrecks and inundated prehistoric sites buried in undisturbed sediments are off limits to collectors of isolated finds. Above all, if you're not sure whether your fossiling location or methods will be legal, make a phone call to the appropriate agency listed in this chapter. Ask questions.

Take copious notes about where you found your more interesting fossils, in case a paleontologist later wants to compare the environment of the find with similar finds in other locales. What was the date of your find? Weather conditions? Was the river high or low, fast flowing or still? What was the geological formation; in other words, what types of sediments were surrounding your find? Shell layers? Black dirt? Blue-green clay? All of this information may be helpful later.

If you find an Indian artifact, such as an arrowhead, the easy—and *illegal*—thing to do is hide it and take it home, and *not* report it. More than likely you'll get away with this. But think of the advantages of reporting your find. First, the point may actually be some missing piece of the puzzle separating two cultures of Native Americans. Or it might be made of a material that doesn't exist in Florida, which may mean it was a traded item from another group of early Americans. What if your point helps prove that trade routes extended from Florida to Eurasia or South America?

Even if your find is a common one, wouldn't it be an honor to know that you're helping science in a small way? Wouldn't a lot more people benefit from the saber-toothed cat skull you uncovered if it was made available to the state museum rather than displayed in your dining room cabinet or sold to a collector?

But what about all the hundreds of thousands of artifacts and fossils stored in boxes in the bowels of museum basements? you ask. What good is it to donate something to science only to see it packed away where no one will ever see it?

Just because there may be boxes and boxes of fossils in some museum basement that haven't been cataloged, cleaned, or assembled, this doesn't necessarily mean that they won't be looked at eventually, as time and funding become available. At least they're safer there than in a creek or cow pasture at the mercy of the elements, or on somebody's mantel where they're handled until they break, or stored away in a shoebox in the attic and forgotten.

Here are some of the laws governing fossil collecting in Florida, followed by those addressing archaeology. Remember that these laws may have changed by the time you read this. It may behoove you to stay up to date.

Paleontology: Florida Fossil Permit

Florida Statutes § 240.516 sets forth the State of Florida's declared intent to protect and preserve vertebrate fossils and vertebrate paleontology sites. All vertebrate fossils found on lands owned or leased by the state belong to the state with title thereto vested in the Florida Museum of Natural History. Field collection of vertebrate fossils may be conducted under the authority of a permit issued by the Program of Vertebrate Paleontology in accordance with FS § 240.516 F.S. and the University of Florida Rule 6C1-7.541 F.A.C. The purpose of the fossil collecting permit is not only to manage this nonrenewable part of Florida's heritage, but to help paleontologists learn more about the range and distribution of the state's fossil animals.

What Areas Are Covered?

The state intends to encourage preservation of its heritage wherever vertebrate fossils are discovered; the state encourages all persons having knowledge of such fossils to notify the Program of Vertebrate Paleontology at the Florida Museum of Natural History. A permit is required for most collecting activities on all lands owned or leased by the state. This includes sites located either on submerged lands or uplands. Please note that existing regulations prohibit collecting in state parks and certain other managed areas. Check the regulations to see if your activities are covered.

What Objects Are Covered?

It is Florida's public policy to protect and preserve all vertebrate fossils, including bones, teeth, natural casts, molds, impressions, and other remains of prehistoric animals. Fossil sharks' teeth are specifically excluded from these regulations, as are fossil plants and invertebrates, including shells, so no permit is required to collect these specimens.

Who May Obtain a Permit?

Any person with an interest in Florida vertebrate fossils may apply for a permit.

Who Must Obtain a Permit?

Any person or entity buying, selling, or trading vertebrate fossils found on or under state-owned or leased land; and/or any person or entity engaged in the systematic collection, acquisition, or restoration of vertebrate fossils found on state-owned or leased land.

"Systematic collection" is hereby characterized by one or more of the following three features:

1. volume of collections of vertebrate fossils in excess of one gallon at one site;
2. use of any power-driven machinery or mechanical excavating tools of any size or hand tools greater than two (2) feet in length;
3. the collection, acquisition, excavation, salvage, exhumation, or restoration of vertebrate fossils at a site on more than three days or a maximum of twenty-four hours during a period of one year.

How Is a Permit Obtained?

Any person wishing to engage in field collection of vertebrate fossils on land owned or leased by the State of Florida should apply for a permit by printing out and completing the application form below [see the section "Florida Fossil Permit Application" later in this chapter] and mailing it to the Florida Program of Vertebrate Paleontology, Florida Museum of Natural History, University of Florida, Gainesville, Florida 32611-7800, U.S.A. The application must be accompanied by a self-identification document such as a copy of the applicant's birth certificate, driver's license, passport, or Social Security card, and a check or money order for $5.00 U.S. made payable to the Program of Vertebrate Paleontology. A permit shall be issued for one year. A multiple-user permit will be granted to an individual representing an organization or institution.

What Obligations Does a Permit Carry?

As a permit holder you can help unlock the secrets of Florida's fossil heritage and preserve this knowledge for future generations. Each year permittees add new discoveries to Florida's fossil heritage. The holder of a permit must report any unusual specimen or unusually rich site to the Program of Vertebrate Paleontology as soon as possible. At any convenient time, no later than the end of the permit year, the permit holder shall submit to the

Program of Vertebrate Paleontology a list of all vertebrate fossils collected during the permit year along with appropriate locality information; or the actual collections with appropriate locality information. If within sixty (60) days of receipt of the list or the actual collection the Program of Vertebrate Paleontology does not request the permittee to donate one or more of the fossils collected, they may be released as "non-essential fossils" to be disposed of however the permit holder may choose.

Questions about Fossil Vertebrates

Direct your questions to:

Russ McCarty   Gainesville, Florida 32611
Program of Vertebrate Paleontology   Tel: (352) 392-1721
Florida Museum of Natural History   E-mail: cormac@flmnh.ufl.edu
University of Florida

Florida Fossil Permit Application

This application is for a permit that will entitle the person named on the permit to collect, for the period of one (1) year, vertebrate fossils on land owned or leased by the State of Florida. The permittee must abide by all the provisions contained in Florida Statutes § 240.516 and the University of Florida Regulation implementing this law.

   Print out and mail completed application to: Program of Vertebrate Paleontology, Florida Museum of Natural History, University of Florida, Gainesville, Florida 32611-7800, U.S.A.

Enclosures with the Application

1. Copy of applicant's identification as stated above;
2. Check or money order for $5.00 in U.S. currency payable to the Program of Vertebrate Paleontology. Please do not send cash.

Applicant's Name:
Address:
Telephone (include area code):
I, the undersigned, affirm that I will abide by Florida Statutes § 240.516 and the Regulations of the Program of Vertebrate Paleontology, University of Florida Rule 6C1-7.541 F.A.C.
Signature:
Date:

Archaeology: Discovering Artifacts in Florida Rivers

Florida has more than 11,000 miles of rivers and streams containing many submerged archaeological sites. Most of these sites are prehistoric camping areas, food preparation sites, resource gathering stations; others are historic landings, mill sites, or fishing camps. The older sites, once on dry land, were drowned when the water level gradually rose after the last Ice Age. Occasionally, sunken watercraft are found in Florida's rivers.

Ownership of Artifacts

Ownership of archaeological sites and artifacts located on state-controlled lands, including submerged lands, is vested in the Division of Historical Resources. The Division's Bureau of Archaeological Research administers policies and programs to protect and interpret these archaeological resources. Written permission to conduct research and recovery activities at state-owned sites must be obtained from the Bureau, except for the recovery of isolated finds in Florida's rivers.

What Is an Isolated Find?

An isolated find is an artifact that has become displaced from its original archaeological context through erosion or water currents. These artifacts, such as prehistoric stone tools and points, coins, bottles, bullets, and other small objects, are not considered of primary archaeological significance, since they have become isolated from their sites of origin.

Isolated finds do not include artifacts associated with sunken or abandoned watercraft, submerged docks, mills, and other structures, or artifacts contained in stratified sites of prehistoric activities. They do not include large artifacts like anchors, and do not include fossils.

Permission to Keep Isolated Finds

Under certain conditions, divers who recover and report the location of isolated finds can obtain ownership of their discoveries from the Division. Isolated finds permission is granted to divers to collect exposed and disassociated artifacts on the surface of state-owned, submerged bottom lands in Florida rivers, except those that are part of state and federal parks, preserves, management areas, or reserves where cultural resources are specifically protected. Artifacts may not be recovered using hand or power tools, or any form of excavation that disturbs the river bottom. Divers who make isolated finds are required to notify the bureau within 30 days of their recovery, with the following written documentation.

Information That Must Be Reported

An Isolated Finds Form should be used to report the following information.

1. Finder's name, address, and telephone number.
2. A map or copy of a map (USGS topographical map or equivalent) plotted to show where the recovery was made, and a verbal description of how to find the location.
3. A description of what was recovered and a photograph or photocopy of the artifact(s) next to a scale (inches or centimeters).

Isolated Finds reports are to be done on a location by location and date by date basis. For example, if a diver makes recoveries from two or more locations on a given date, reports on each recovery location are required. Likewise, if a diver makes recoveries from the same location on different dates, reports for each recovery day are required. It is the diver's obligation to complete this reporting process within 30 days of a find. This information should be sent to:

Isolated Finds
Bureau of Archaeological Research
R. A. Gray Building, Room 312
500 South Bronough Street
Tallahassee, FL 32399-0250
Phone (850) 487-2299

When Is Ownership Transferred to the Finder?

Once the finder has provided the information about the isolated find, the Division will notify the finder it has received the report. The Division has 90 days from the date it receives the information to determine the disposition of the isolated find.

The Division may transfer ownership to the finder. The Division may determine that a particular artifact needs to be studied, cast, or otherwise documented in more detail before returning it to the finder. Or, in some instances, the Division may retain possession of the original artifact and may provide the finder with a replica. If, after the 90-day period, the Division has not notified the finder of its intent, ownership of the artifact is automatically transferred to the finder.

Previously Collected Finds

To apply for legal ownership of past isolated finds, use the same Isolated Finds Form and follow the instructions above. Artifacts recovered at any time in the past may be reported at any time in the future.

Guidelines for Isolated Artifacts Recovered from State-owned River Bottoms

The Division of Historical Resources holds title under Chapter 267 to archaeological remains and artifacts on state-owned lands, including submerged lands like rivers and streams. To protect state-owned archaeological sites from damage, the law prohibits disturbance of sites and collection of artifacts without the Division's permission.

Certain classess of archaeological remains do not warrant such strict control and may be collected under certain circumstances. The following guidelines describe a program of isolated finds managed by the Division of Historical Resources under which permission is granted to recover artifacts in exchange for information about them.

Terms used in these guidelines have the following meanings:

Archaeological association means the relationship among artifacts that are in original, or stratified context within an archaeological site.

Archaeological significance means capable of providing scientific or humanistic understandings of past human behavior, cultural adaptation, and related topics through the application of scientific or scholarly techniques such as controlled observation, contextual measurement, controlled collection, analysis, interpretation, and explanation.

Archaeological site means a location with intact archaeological deposits in original or stratified archaeological association and containing physical evidence of human habitation, occupation, use, or activity, which are at least 50 years of age and which include the context in which such evidence is situated.

Artifact means an object made, modified, or used by people and which is at least 50 years of age; modern coins and jewelry that have been lost are not considered within this definition of artifact.

Commercial exchange or sale means transfer of ownership of artifacts from one private owner to the other for a consideration with the purpose of conducting a business or making a profit.

Intact archaeological deposit means archaeological remains that retain their original, or stratified association within an archaeological site.

Isolated artifact for purposes of this chapter means an artifact that has been previously displaced from its original archaeological association, that is no longer part of an archaeological site, and that has little or no archaeological significance as an object in itself.

Examples of isolated artifacts include stone tools such as projectile points, knives, scrapers, and cores; bone awls, coins, bottles, bullets, or other relatively small artifacts meeting the criteria of isolation in this definition.

State-owned sovereignty submerged bottoms of inland waters means the bottoms of navigable inland waterways such as rivers, streams, lakes, and ponds that are owned by the State of Florida.

Guidelines Establishing the Scope of the Isolated Finds Policy

1. Permission to recover isolated artifacts is limited to state-owned bottoms of inland waterways. It does not extend to adjacent upland property owned by the state above the mean high water line. It does not extend to sovereignty submerged lands in the Atlantic Ocean or Gulf of Mexico or to their non-fresh water estuaries, bays, lagoons, or inlets.

2. Permission to recover isolated artifacts is limited to collection by hand only; no tools useable for digging, dredging, or excavating can be used to recover isolated artifacts.

3. Permission to recover isolated artifacts does not extend to submerged lands within the boundaries of public lands managed under authorities that include protection of archaeological remains, such as units of the Florida Park Service, the Florida Aquatic Preserve System, the National Park Service, the National Marine Sanctuary System, the National Seashore System, the National Wildlife Refuge System, and county or municipal parks and preserves.

4. Permission to recover isolated artifacts does not extend to known or recorded archaeological sites where multiple artifacts exist in an intact archaeological deposit in meaningful archaeological association. Such archaeological sites may be posted by the Division to show that permission

to recover isolated artifacts does not apply within the limited areas so marked.

Important Notice: Isolated Finds may NOT be recovered from river channel segments located inside Federal and State Parks, Reserves, Preserves or Management areas.

Code of Ethics

The Florida Paleontological Society has had in place for over 20 years a code of ethics for its members:

- Members are expected to respect all private and public properties.
- No member shall collect without appropriate permission on private or public properties.
- Members should make a sincere effort to keep themselves informed of laws, regulations, and rules on collecting on private or public properties.
- Members shall not use firearms, blasting equipment, or dredging apparatuses without appropriate licenses and permits.
- Members shall dispose of litter properly.
- Members shall report to proper state offices any seemingly important paleontological or archaeological sites.
- Members shall respect and cooperate with field trip leaders or designated authorities in all collecting areas.
- Members shall appreciate and protect our heritage of natural resources.
- Members shall conduct themselves in a manner that best represents FPS.

Epilogue

Need Therapy? Try Fossil Hunting

There is nothing quite as therapeutic to me as fossil hunting. It doesn't matter how stressful a week I've had; when I take to the bone beds, it's all behind me. While I'm out, I'm not just looking for old bones. I have come across owls, otters, bobcats, manatees, alligators, snakes, and the tracks of the endangered Florida panther. I've been frightened a couple of times, but mostly I have been in awe of the beauty of nature as it appears to have unfolded over the eons.

I've leaned against an old-growth cypress tree that a Calusa Indian may well have leaned against 500 years earlier. I've stood in the exact spot where Florida's largest land animal—a 20-foot giant ground sloth—lived and died a million years before that. Picking up one of its huge claws, I wonder if I am the first human ever to see this particular creature. What was life like for her, and how did she meet her death? I've sat next to a 10-million-year-old fossilized sea cow and tried to imagine what our state and our planet was like at the time.

It's easy to feel as if you've stepped back in time in Florida's ancient-looking creeks. Photo by Marisa Renz.

Fossiling helps me understand that even though we would like to think we humans are the most important life forms on Earth, we may be far from it. We may think we're the dominant species, but there are creatures that have survived on this third rock from the sun for hundreds of millions of years, and that will probably be here at least that much longer after the human race has expired. There are trees older today than any living person, insects more complex, animals more content, and microscopic germs stronger. Quite possibly, the only thing we have that other beings lack is a tremendous ego.

Fossiling doesn't have to be only for scientists. It can be something that people like you and me can appreciate and learn from—even teach to others. We don't have to be experts to discover and share the wonderful world of the past.

Now, go find your own bones!

Some visitors don't look very friendly, such as this golden orb weaver at home above many of Florida's creeks. Photo by author.

You never know when you'll encounter a friendly visitor. Photo by author.

This owl landed above me and watched curiously as I searched for fossils. Photo by author.

Florida Fossiling Clubs

There are some wonderful amateur paleontology and archaeology/anthropology clubs in Florida to help you get started. Here are a few; keep in mind that by the time you read this book, they will probably have new officers. In that case, check with the Florida Museum of Natural History in Gainesville, (352) 392-1721, and see if it has up-to-date information.

Paleontology Clubs

Bone Valley Fossil Society, Lakeland, Fla. Contact Mary Harris, 130 E. Johnson Avenue, #205, Lake Wales, Fla. 33853.
Ed Metrin, editor, (813) 321-7462.
Florida Fossil Hunters, Orlando, Fla. Contact Dave Dunaway, president, (407) 293-0726.
Florida Paleontological Society, Gainesville, Fla. Contact Eric Taylor, FPS, Florida Museum of Natural History, University of Florida, Gainesville, Fla. 32611.
Fossil Expeditions Guide Service, Fort Myers, Fla. Contact Mark Renz, 213 Lincoln Avenue, Lehigh Acres, Fla. 33972. E-mail: Fossilx@earthlink.net.
Tampa Bay Fossil Club, Tampa, Fla. Contact Frank Kocsis, Jr., 2913 Fairfield Court, Palm Harbor, Fla. 34683. Phone: (813) 725-1650.

Archaeology/Anthropology Clubs

Regional Chapters of the Florida Anthropological Society, P.O. Box 5142, Gainesville, Fla. 32602:
Apalachee Archaeological Society—Tampa
Archaeological Society of Southern Florida—Tallahassee
Broward County Archaeological Society—Miami
Central Florida Anthropological Society—Fort Lauderdale
Central Gulf Coast Archaeological Society—Tampa
Indian River Anthropological Society—Titusville
Kissimmee Valley Archaeological and Historical Conservancy—Sebring
Northeast Florida Anthropological Society—Jacksonville
Pensacola Archaeological Society—Pensacola
St. Augustine Archaeological Society—St. Augustine
Southwest Florida Archaeological Society—Naples
Timesifters Archaeological Society—Sarasota
Volusia Anthropological Society—Ormond Beach

Bibliography

Aucilla River Times, February 1995–March 1998.

Brayfield, Lelia, and William Brayfield
   1993   *Fossil Shells: A Guide for Identifying Fossil Shells and Other Invertebrates.* 3rd ed.
          Gainesville, Fla.: Florida Paleontological Society.

Brodkorb, Pierce
   1963   "A Giant Flightless Bird from the Pleistocene of Florida." *Auk* 80, no. 2: 11–115.

Brown, Robin C.
   1988   *Florida's Fossils: Guide to Location, Identification, and Enjoyment.* Sarasota, Fla.:
          Pineapple Press.
   1994   *Florida's First People.* Sarasota, Fla.: Pineapple Press.

California Academy of Sciences
   1995   *California Wild on the Line.* California Wild/Pacific Discovery Archives. Internet:
          www.calacademy.org/pacdis/magamenu.htm

Carroll, Robert L.
   1968   *Vertebrate Paleontology and Evolution.* New York: Freeman.

Case, Gerard R.
   1973   *Fossil Sharks: A Pictorial Review.* New York: Pioneer Light.
   1982   *A Pictorial Guide to Fossils.* New York: Van Nostrand Reinhold.

Code of Ethics
   1997   *Florida Paleontological Society, Inc. Newsletter* 14, no. 3 (Summer).

Colbert, Edwin H.
   1980   *A Fossil-Hunter's Notebook.* New York: Elsevier-Dutton.

Dew, Douglas K., M.D.
   1996   "The Paleo Doctor." *Tampa Bay Fossil Chronicles* (March): 112–14.

Garcia, Frank A.
   1974   *Illustrated Guide to Fossil Vertebrates.* Apollo Beach, Fla.: Garcia Paleontology.
   1993   *Miracle at Cockroach Bay . . . The Leisey Shell Fossils.* Apollo Beach, Fla.: Garcia
          Paleontology.

Glaros, Lou, and Doug Spar
   1987   *A Canoeing and Kayaking Guide to the Streams of Florida.* Vols. 1 and 2. Birming-
          ham, Ala.: Manasha Ridge Press.

Kocsis, Frank Jr.
   1998   *Vertebrate Fossils: A Neophyte's Guide.* Palm Harbor, Fla.: IBIS Graphics.

Kozuch, Laura
   1993   "Sharks and Shark Products in Prehistoric South Florida." Master's thesis, Insti-
          tute of Archaeology and Paleoenvironmental Studies, monograph no. 2, Univer-
          sity of Florida.

Krystek, Lee
   1998   *Museum of Unnatural History.* Home page, Internet, Krystek@unmuseum.mus
          .pa.us/

Kurten, Bjorn
   1971   *The Age of Mammals.* New York: Columbia University Press.
   1980   *Pleistocene Mammals of North America.* New York: Columbia University Press.

Lister, Adrian, and Paul Bahn
    1994. *Mammoths*. New York: Macmillan.
MacFadden, Bruce J.
    1994   *Fossil Horses: Systematics, Paleobiology, and Evolution of the Family Equidae*. New York: Cambridge University Press.
Miles, Gilbert
    1990   *Mammalian Osteology*. Columbia, Mo.: Missouri Archaeological Society.
Olsen, S. J.
    1963   *Fossil Mammals of Florida*. Florida Bureau of Geology, Tallahassee, special publication no. 6.
Papers of the Peabody Museum of Archaeology and Ethnology
    1972   Vol. 56, no. 3. Cambridge, Mass.: Harvard University Press.
Plaster Jacket
    1979   No. 32 (October). Florida Museum of Natural History, Gainesville.
Reader's Digest
    1986   *Sharks: Silent Hunters of the Deep*. Reader's Digest (Australia).
Renz, Mark
    Fossil Expeditions (bimonthly newsletter). Lehigh Acres, Fla.
Rohmer, Alfred S.
    1966   *Vertebrate Paleontology*. Chicago: University of Chicago Press.
Savage, R. J. G., and M. R. Long
    1989   *Mammal Evolution: An Illustrated Guide*. New York: Facts on File Publications.
Searfoss, Glen
    1995   *Skulls and Bones: A Guide to the Skeletal Structures and Behaviors of North American Mammals*. Mechanicsburg: Stackpole Books.
Simpson, George G.
    1984   *Fossils and the History of Life*. New York: Freeman.
Sinibaldi, Robert W.
    1998   *Fossil Diving in Florida's Waters or Any Other Waters Containing Prehistoric Treasures*. Palm Harbor, Fla.: IBIS Graphics.
Sleeper, Barbara
    1996   *Beneath the Blackwater: Alligators*. Northworld Wildlife Series. Minocqua, Wis.: Northwind Press.
Thomas, M. C.
    1992   *Fossil Vertebrates: Beach and Bank Collecting for Amateurs*. Rev. ed. Gainesville, Fla.: Florida Paleontological Society.
Turner, Alan
    1997   *The Big Cats and Their Fossil Relatives*. New York: Columbia University Press.
Webb, S. David
    1968   *Underwater Paleontology of Florida's Rivers*. National Geographic Society Research Reports, 479–81.
    1974   *Pleistocene Mammals of Florida*. Gainesville, Fla.: University Press of Florida.
Webb, S. David, and Kenneth Wilkins
    1983   *Historical Biogeography of Florida Pleistocene Mammals*. Special publication. Pittsburgh: Carnegie Museum of Natural History, no. 8, 370–83.